ESPAÑOL ESENCIAL 1

Fundamentals of Spanish

Stephen L. Levy

Former Head, Foreign Language Department
Roslyn (New York) Public Schools

AMSCO SCHOOL PUBLICATIONS, INC.
315 Hudson Street/New York, N.Y. 10013

To Martin, Elaine, Michelle, Allison, Jeremy, Morgan, and Emma, with love.

Text and Cover Design by A Good Thing, Inc.
Illustrations by Felipe Galindo

Please visit our Web site at:
www.amscopub.com

When ordering this book, please specify *either* **R 736 W** *or*
ESPAÑOL ESENCIAL 1: FUNDAMENTALS OF SPANISH

ISBN   1-56765-484-3

NYC Item   56765-484-2

Printed in the United States

1 2 3 4 5 6 7 8 9 10   09 08 07 06 05 04 03

Preface

Español Esencial 1 has been prepared for students who are in their first year of Spanish language study. It offers a comprehensive review and thorough understanding of the elements of the Spanish language that are generally covered in a first-year course. It can be used as a complement/supplement to any basal textbook series or solely for review and additional practice.

ORGANIZATION

Español Esencial 1 contains 18 chapters that are organized around related grammar topics. For ease of study and use, concise and clear explanations of the grammatical concepts are presented and are followed by examples that illustrate the concepts. Care has been taken to avoid the use of complex structural elements and to present the practice exercises through contexts that are found in daily usage of the language.

EXERCISES

To maximize efficiency in learning, the exercises follow the grammatical explanations and examples. In order that the practice provided by the exercises be meaningful and lead the student to use the language in a real-life communicative manner, the exercises are set in contexts that are both functional and realistic. Many of the exercises are also personalized to stimulate original student response and meaningful assimilation and internalization of the concepts under study. These exercises lend themselves to both oral and written practice of the language based on linguistic and visual cues. The last exercise in each chapter is open-ended to provide students with the opportunity to express themselves and to voice their personal opinions in Spanish, within the scope of the concept under study.

VOCABULARY

The vocabulary found in this book has been carefully controlled and is systematically recycled throughout subsequent chapters. The vocabulary topics are those found most frequently in a first-year Spanish course. Where more extended or broader vocabulary is used in an exercise, a section called **Para Expresarse Mejor**, in which the vocabulary for the exercise is presented, precedes it. A Spanish-English vocabulary is included at the end of the book.

FLEXIBILITY AND OTHER FEATURES

The topical organization and the concise explanations followed by examples found in each chapter permit the teacher to follow any sequence suitable to the needs of the students and the objectives of the course. This flexibility is facilitated by the detailed table of contents at the front of the book. The Appendix features complete model verb tables and the principal parts of common irregular verbs that are covered in the book as well as basic rules of Spanish punctuation, syllabication, and stress.

Both students and teachers will find the organization and layout of the book to be easy to follow and suitable and flexible to their individual needs. Its basic design is to facilitate communicative use of the language while mastering the basic structures that are needed for meaningful communication to occur.

The Author

Contents

CHAPTER 1
Present Tense of -AR Verbs

1. In Spanish, all verbs belong to a family of verbs or conjugation that is determined by the infinitive ending: *ar*, *er*, or *-ir*.

2. The present tense of regular -*ar* verbs is formed by dropping the infinitive ending -*ar* and adding the personal endings -*o*, -*as*, -*a*, -*amos*, -*áis*, -*an* to the stem.

comprar *to buy*			
yo	compro	nosotros, -as	compramos
tú	compras	vosotros, -as	compráis
Ud., él, ella	compra	Uds., ellos, ellas	compran

3. The present tense in Spanish is equivalent to the present tense in English.

Ud. compra   *you buy, you're buying, you do buy*

ella compra   *she buys, she's buying, she does buy*

NOTE: 1. The subject pronouns *yo, tú, él, ella, nosotros, vosotros, ellos,* and *ellas* are generally omitted because the verb endings identify the doer of the action. These subjects are usually included for clarity, emphasis, or contrast. The subject pronouns *usted* (*Ud.*) and *ustedes* (*Uds.*) are usually expressed in Spanish.

Uds. **hablan francés.**   *You speak French.*

Yo **hablo alemán también.**   *I speak German also.*

Tú **hablas inglés pero Ana habla japonés.**   *You speak English but Ana speaks Japanese.*

2. The feminine forms of *nosotros* and *vosotros* are *nosotras* and *vosotras*.

3. The familiar forms, *tú* and *vosotros*, are used when addressing close relatives, intimate friends, small children, or pets. In most Spanish-American countries the *ustedes* form is used instead of the *vosotros* form.

4. The present tense can also refer to the future, provided that another sentence element identifies the future time.

El señor *viaja* mañana.   *The man is traveling tomorrow.*

Regresamos el domingo.   *We'll return on Sunday.*

5. Questions can be formed in Spanish by placing the subject after the verb or at the end of the sentence. In speaking, changing the intonation of the sentence can make the statement into a question.

¿ Trabaja José **en casa?**   *Does José work at home?*

¿ Viaja **mucho *tu padre*?**   *Does your father travel a lot?*

¿Ella trabaja en la corte?   *She works in the court?*

6. A verb is made negative by placing *no* before it.

Yo *no* canto en el coro.	*I don't sing in the chorus.*
Elena *no* desea estudiar hoy.	*Helen doesn't want to study today.*

1. Common -*AR* Verbs

arreglar	*to arrange, fix*	**lavar**	*to wash*
ayudar	*to help*	**llamar**	*to call*
bailar	*to dance*	**llegar**	*to arrive*
bajar	*to go down, descend; to lower*	**llevar**	*to carry, take; to wear*
buscar	*to look for*	**mirar**	*to look at*
caminar	*to walk*	**montar**	*to ride (a bicycle, horse)*
cantar	*to sing*	**nadar**	*to swim*
celebrar	*to celebrate*	**necesitar**	*to need*
cocinar	*to cook*	**pagar**	*to pay (for)*
comprar	*to buy*	**pasar**	*to pass; to spend (time)*
contestar	*to answer*	**patinar**	*to skate*
decorar	*to decorate*	**practicar**	*to practice*
desear	*to wish, want*	**preguntar**	*to ask*
dibujar	*to draw*	**preparar**	*to prepare*
enseñar	*to teach*	**regresar**	*to return*
entrar (en)	*to enter (into)*	**sacar**	*to take out; to take (photo)*
escuchar	*to listen (to)*	**terminar**	*to finish, end*
esperar	*to wait; to hope*	**tocar**	*to touch; to play (a musical instrument)*
estudiar	*to study*	**tomar**	*to take; to drink*
explicar	*to explain*	**trabajar**	*to work*
ganar	*to win*	**usar**	*to use; to wear*
gritar	*to shout*	**viajar**	*to travel*
hablar	*to speak*	**visitar**	*to visit*
invitar	*to invite*		

EXERCISE A   **Los deportes**   Tell what sport each of the following people practices.

EXAMPLE: Alberto / el tenis   Alberto **practica** el tenis.

1. Estela / el fútbol _____

2. Gabriel y yo / el béisbol _____

3. tú / el baloncesto _____

4. Laura e Inés / la natación _____

5. Uds. / la lucha libre _____

6. yo / el patinaje _____

EXERCISE B   **Después de las clases** Gladys describes what she and her friends do after school. Complete the statements.

EXAMPLE: Pilar / mirar la televisión   Pilar **mira** la televisión.

1. Jorge y yo / caminar en el parque   _____

2. Valerie / preparar la tarea   _____

3. tú / trabajar en un restaurante   _____

4. yo / visitar a mi abuela   _____

5. Cameron y Jack / estudiar en la biblioteca   _____

6. Nancy / cuidar a su hermanito   _____

7. Rafa / ayudar a su madre en casa   _____

EXERCISE C   **Un mensaje electrónico** Sally sends this message to her host family in Costa Rica. Complete her message with the appropriate form of the verbs indicated.

Queridos amigos:

Yo _____ mañana. El vuelo 901, en que yo _____ , _____ al
　　　1. (llegar)　　　　　　　　　　　　　　　　　　2. (viajar)　　　　　3. (llegar)

aeropuerto internacional a las tres de la tarde. Otros chicos de mi escuela _____
　　　　　　　　　　　　　　　　　　　　　　　　　　　　　　　　　　　4. (viajar)

en el mismo vuelo pero ellos _____ a otras familias. Es la primera vez que yo
　　　　　　　　　　　　　　5. (visitar)

no _____ a mis padres en las vacaciones. Yo _____ verlos en el aero-
　　6. (acompañar)　　　　　　　　　　　　　　　　　7. (esperar)

puerto. Nosotros _____ un taxi para ir a su casa. Yo no _____ mucho
　　　　　　　　8. (tomar)　　　　　　　　　　　　　　　9. (llevar)

en la maleta porque yo _____ comprar muchas cosas durante mi visita.
　　　　　　　　　　　　10. (desear)

Hasta mañana.

Sally

EXERCISE D | **De compras** Answer the questions that the salesperson asks you during a shopping trip for beach wear. Use the following vocabulary in your answers.

PARA EXPRESARSE MEJOR
De compras *Shopping*

la talla *size*
el número *shoe size*
chico, -a *small*
mediano, -a *medium*
grande *large*
la prenda de ropa *article of clothing*

la tarjeta de crédito *credit card*
al contado *cash*
el traje de baño *bathing suit*
los pantalones cortos *shorts*
el sombrero *hat*
las sandalias *sandals*

1. ¿Qué busca Ud.?

   _____

2. ¿Que talla usa Ud.?

   _____

3. ¿Qué color desea Ud.?

   _____

4. ¿Necesita Ud. otra cosa?

   _____

5. ¿Paga Ud. al contado o con una tarjeta de crédito?

   _____

EXERCISE E | **Actividades** Alan is talking about the activities he and his friends spend time doing. Combine the elements to tell who does what.

yo	nadar en la piscina
tú	trabajar en el periódico escolar
Elvira	escuchar música
Antonio	mirar las telenovelas
Luke y yo	dibujar caricaturas
Mario y Fred	montar en bicicleta
Josh y Lupe	tocar la guitarra
Luisa	hablar por teléfono

1. _____

2. _____

3. _____

4. _____

5. _____

6. _____

7. _____

8. _____

EXERCISE F   **Preguntas**   Max isn't sure who does these activities. Express the questions he asks.

EXAMPLE: Vinny / practicar el béisbol

¿**Practica** Vinny el béisbol?   OR   ¿**Practica** el béisbol Vinny?

1. Sarita / estudiar informática

_____

2. Manuel y Hans / caminar en el parque

_____

3. tú / patinar en hielo

_____

4. Alex / tocar el piano

_____

5. Jim y Aniluz / bailar

_____

6. yo / escuchar el radio portátil

_____

EXERCISE G   **Más preguntas**   A recently arrived exchange student from Chile wants to know more about you and your friends. Express the questions he asked for these responses.

EXAMPLE: Guillermo y Victoria hablan español.   ¿**Hablan** español Guillermo y Victoria?

1. Johnny estudia porque desea pasar el examen.

_____

2. Uds. estudian un idioma extranjero.

_____

3. Tú y yo deseamos mirar el partido de fútbol en la televisión.

_____

4. Los hermanos Wong trabajan en el supermercado.

_____

5. Jenny y su hermana necesitan comprar otra computadora.

_____

6. Yo practico el tenis cada tarde.

_____

7. Tú caminas una milla todos los días.

_____

EXERCISE H   **De malas**   Robert responds negatively to everything he is asked when he is in a bad mood and doesn't want to be bothered. Express Robert's answers.

EXAMPLE: ¿Deseas mirar las fotos de la fiesta?   **No, no deseo** mirar las fotos de la fiesta.

1. ¿Compra Luis una bicicleta nueva?

_____

2. ¿Bailan bien Lenny y Gloria?

_____

3. ¿Desean Uds. cenar en un restaurante después de la película?

_____

4. ¿Necesitas tú visitar un museo para la clase de arte?

_____

5. ¿Prepara tu mamá la comida para la fiesta?

_____

6. ¿Toca Miguel un instrumento musical?

_____

7. ¿Estudias tú todos los días?

_____

EXERCISE I   **En las clases**   Tell what you and your classmates don't do in your classes.

EXAMPLE: Pedro / sacar fotografías en la clase de inglés
        Pedro **no saca** fotografías en la clase de inglés.

1. Marisol / hablar por teléfono en la clase de arte

_____

2. ellos / nadar en la clase de biología

_____

3. tú / cocinar en la clase de matemáticas

_____

4. Gwen y yo / montar en bicicleta en la clase de español

_____

5. yo / tocar el violín en la clase de historia

_____

6. Uds. / escuchar música en la clase de educación física

_____

EXERCISE J   **Muchas preguntas**   You are in a new school and some of your old friends visit you. A new friend asks you questions about yourself and your old friends. Answer the questions as indicated.

EXAMPLE: ¿Pasas tú mucho tiempo en la cafetería de la escuela?   (no)
      No, no paso mucho tiempo en la cafetería de la escuela.

1. ¿Sacas tú muchas fotografías de tu familia?   (sí)

_____

2. ¿Visitas tú a tus otros amigos?   (no)

_____

3. ¿Trabajan tus amigos por la tarde?   (no)

_____

4. ¿Escuchan Uds. la música clásica?   (no)

_____

5. ¿Toman Pepe y Tito el autobús escolar?   (no)

_____

6. ¿Necesitas comprar algo en el centro comercial?   (sí)

_____

7. ¿Deseas contestar más preguntas?   (no)

_____

EXERCISE K   **Datos personales**   Using verbs from the list of common -ar verbs, prepare five questions you would ask a newly arrived exchange student at your school about him/herself.

1. _____
2. _____
3. _____
4. _____
5. _____

| EXERCISE L | **Amigos por correspondencia**   Prepare a letter of six sentences that you will post on the school's Web site. Talk about yourself and your hope of finding an electronic pen pal. |

_____

_____

_____

_____

_____

_____

CHAPTER 2
The Present Tense of -ER and -IR Verbs

1. The Present Tense of -ER Verbs

a. The present tense of regular -er verbs is formed by dropping the infinitive ending -er and adding the personal endings -o, -es, -e, -emos, -éis, -en to the stem.

vender *to sell*			
yo	vendo	nosotros, -as	vendemos
tú	vendes	vosotros, -as	vendéis
Ud., él, ella	vende	Uds., ellos, ellas	venden

b. The present tense in Spanish is equivalent to the present tense in English.

tú vendes   *you sell, you're selling, you do sell*

ellos venden   *they sell, they're selling, they do sell*

2. Common -ER Verbs

aprender *to learn*

beber *to drink*

comer *to eat*

comprender *to understand*

correr *to run*

creer *to believe*

deber + infinitive *ought, should; to be supposed to*

leer *to read*

prometer *to promise*

responder *to answer*

| EXERCISE A | **La sed** (Thirst) Tell what each person drinks during a rest stop on a sightseeing tour.

EXAMPLE: Ud. / agua mineral   Ud. **bebe** agua mineral.

1. Jack y Tom / jugo de naranja   _____

2. yo / un refresco   _____

3. el guía / café   _____

4. tú / un chocolate caliente   _____

5. los niños / un batido de fresa   _____

6. mi hermana y yo / un té helado   _____

7. Selena / una limonada   _____

| EXERCISE B | **Todos comprenden.** Tell which language these people understand. |

EXAMPLE: Estela / el español   Estela **comprende** el español.

1. Kyoko / el japonés   _____

2. Laura y Enzo / el italiano   _____

3. Ivan / el ruso   _____

4. yo / el inglés   _____

5. tú / el francés   _____

6. Kurt y yo / el alemán   _____

| EXERCISE C | **Obligaciones** Tell what Larry's father says everyone should be doing. |

EXAMPLE: Cynthia / sacar al perro   Cynthia **debe** sacar al perro.

1. tu mamá / preparar la comida   _____

2. yo / lavar el carro   _____

3. tus hermanos / recoger los juguetes   _____

4. tú / preparar la tarea   _____

5. Vicente / llegar a casa temprano   _____

6. tu mamá y yo / ir de compras   _____

| EXERCISE D | **Comentarios escolares** Express the comments Jane makes about her math class. |

EXAMPLE: El profesor / creer / nosotros somos matemáticos
El profesor **cree** que nosotros somos matemáticos.

1. Gregorio / aprender / la lección fácilmente

_____

2. yo / prometer / estudiar más

_____

3. Elvira y yo / leer / los problemas juntas

_____

4. tú / comprender / bien la lección

_____

5. Alberto / responder / a todas las preguntas

_____

6. Juan y Kim / creer / la lección es difícil

_____

EXERCISE E   **Todos hacen algo.**   Tell what each of these people is doing.

EXAMPLE: la abuela / beber té caliente   La abuela **bebe** té caliente.

1. Jorge / correr en una carrera

_____

2. tú y yo / leer novelas románticas

_____

3. ellos / responder a los anuncios

_____

4. tú / aprender el japonés

_____

5. el señor Limones / vender carros nuevos

_____

6. mi hermano / prometer estudiar más

_____

7. Uds. / comer comida exótica

_____

8. yo / comprender los problemas complejos

_____

EXERCISE F   **Los niños aprenden.**   Nora wrote a paragraph about children. Complete the paragraph with the appropriate form of the verb indicated.

Cada día un bebé _____ algo nuevo. Primero los niños _____ leche
                  1. (aprender)   2. (beber)

y luego ellos _____ poco a poco. Los bebés _____ mucho y a veces
             3. (comer)   4. (comprender)

ellos _____ con sonrisas o llanto. Al tener un año de edad, muchos niños
     5. (responder)

ya _____ . En las tiendas _____ muchos libros infantiles y pronto los
   6. (correr)   7. (vender)

niños _____ también. Los padres _____ prestar mucha atención a
     8. (leer)   9. (deber)

los niños.

3.   The Present Tense of Regular *-IR* Verbs

a. The present tense of regular *-ir* verbs is formed by dropping the infinitive ending *-ir* and adding the personal endings *-o, -es, -e, -imos, -ís, -en* to the stem.

cubrir *to cover*			
yo	cub**ro**	nosotros, -as	cub**rimos**
tú	cub**res**	vosotros, -as	cub**rís**
Ud., él, ella	cub**re**	Uds., ellos, ellas	cub**ren**

b. The present tense in Spanish is equivalent to the present tense in English.

yo cubro   *I cover, I'm covering, I do cover*

Ud. cubre   *you cover, you're covering, you do cover*

4.   Common *-IR* Verbs

asistir (a) *to attend*

decidir *to decide*

describir *to describe*

descubrir *to discover*

dividir *to divide*

escribir *to write*

insistir (en) *to insist (on)*

partir *to leave, depart*

permitir *to permit, allow*

recibir *to receive*

subir *to go up, climb; to raise*

sufrir *to suffer*

vivir *to live*

EXERCISE G   **Decisiones** Tell what each of the following people decides to do during the summer vacation.

EXAMPLE: el señor Gómez / viajar a Puerto Rico
El señor Gómez **decide** viajar a Puerto Rico.

1. Cathy / trabajar en la biblioteca

   _____

2. Ted y Felipe / ir a la playa todos los días

   _____

3. mi papá / pintar la casa

   _____

4. yo / leer muchos libros

   _____

5. tú / correr en el parque por la mañana

   _____

6. Lucy y yo / ver muchas películas

   _____

EXERCISE H   **Ubicaciones** Joey is trying to visualize where his classmates live. Tell where they live using a different expression for each classmate.

PARA EXPRESARSE MEJOR
Ubicaciones *Locations*

cerca de *near*	**al lado de** *next to*
lejos de *far from*	**detrás de** *behind*
frente a *facing*	**delante de** *in front of*
entre *between*	

EXAMPLE: Lisa / el centro comercial   Lisa **vive cerca del** centro comercial.

1. tú / la escuela   _____

2. Andy y Greg / el club deportivo   _____

3. Mirta y yo / el cine   _____

4. Laura / el parque   _____

5. yo / el banco   _____

6. Uds. / el supermercado   _____

EXERCISE I   **Destinos** Everyone in the Beltrán family has a different destination today. Tell what each of them attends.

EXAMPLE: el señor Beltrán / un congreso   El señor Beltrán **asiste a** un congreso.

1. los abuelos / una boda   _____

2. Pepito y yo / un partido de fútbol   _____

3. la señora Beltrán / una comida   _____

4. tú / una asamblea escolar   _____

5. Victoria / una clase de ejercicios físicos   _____

6. yo / el ensayo del coro   _____

EXERCISE J   **El parque de bomberos** Victor is very excited about his class's visit to the local fire house. Express what he says about the school trip. Refer to the vocabulary below, if necessary.

PARA EXPRESARSE MEJOR

El parque de bomberos *The firehouse*

bombero(-era) *firefighter*   **el incendio** *fire*

comandante (m. & f.) *commander, chief*   **la máscara** *mask*

el peligro *danger*   **el camión de bomberos** *fire truck*

el perro dálmata *Dalmatian dog*

EXAMPLE: el director / permitir la excursión escolar
El director **permite** la excursión escolar.

1. el autobús / salir a las diez y media

   _____

2. la maestra / dividir la clase en grupos

   _____

3. Gladys y yo / insistir en estar en el mismo grupo

   _____

4. los alumnos / descubrir muchas cosas importantes

   _____

5. el comandante / describir los peligros de un incendio

   _____

6. cada alumno / recibir una lección

   _____

7. dos perros dálmatas / vivir en el parque de bomberos

   _____

8. tú / subir al camión de los bomberos

   _____

9. yo / cubrir la cara con una máscara de oxígeno

   _____

10. todos los alumnos / escribir una carta de gracias

    _____

EXERCISE K   **Nunca más** (Never again)   When her parents return home, Randy describes her first experience babysitting her younger brothers and sister. Express her description of the children's behavior.

EXAMPLE: Gregorio y Miguel / abrir la puerta   Gregorio y Miguel **abren** la puerta.

1. los niños / salir a la calle

   _____

2. el gato / subir a la mesa

_____

3. yo / insistir en mirar la televisión

_____

4. los niños y yo / asistir a la barbacoa de un vecino

_____

5. Miguel / cubrir a su hermano con una toalla

_____

6. Gregorio y Elsa / escribir en la pared con marcadores

_____

7. yo / decidir no hacer esto otra vez

_____

5. *-ER* and *-IR* Verbs in Negative and Interrogative Constructions

a. A verb is made negative by placing *no* before it.

Ella *no* recibe correo electrónico.	*She doesn't receive e-mail.*
Ustedes *no* responden inmediatamente.	*You don't answer immediately.*

b. In Spanish questions can be formed by placing the subject after the verb or at the end of the sentence. In speaking, changing the intonation of the sentence can make the statement into a question.

¿Responden Uds. **a la pregunta?**	*Do you answer the question?*
¿Beben **refresco** *los niños?*	*Do the children drink soda?*
¿Mari insiste en pagar la cuenta?	*Does Mari insist on paying the bill?*

EXERCISE L   **Mil veces no** (A thousand times no)   Martin never agrees with anything he hears. Express what he says about the following information.

EXAMPLE: La tierra cubre las nubes.   La tierra **no cubre** las nubes.

1. El lechero vende fruta.

_____

2. Las vacas beben leche.

_____

3. Los científicos descubren nuevas reglas gramaticales.

_____

4. Un pintor describe un paisaje con palabras.

_____

5. Los barcos parten del aeropuerto.

_____

6. Mi abuelo lee las noticias en el radio.

_____

| EXERCISE M | **Estamos confundidos.** (We're confused.)   You are telling your family about some people at school. They are confused by what you say and ask questions. Express their questions. |

EXAMPLE: Ralph y Eduardo comen en el sótano de la escuela.
           ¿Comen Ralph y Eduardo en el sótano de la escuela?

1. Juan Carlos comprende el chino.

_____

2. Selena bebe refresco en la clase.

_____

3. Felipe y yo corremos durante la hora de recreo.

_____

4. Melissa asiste a las clases de su gemela.

_____

5. La maestra escribe en la pizarra con tiza azul.

_____

6. Kevin y Rebecca viven en otra parte de la ciudad.

_____

7. Yo aprendo a bailar en la clase de educación física.

_____

| EXERCISE N | **Un día ordinario**   Using as many of the verbs in this chapter as possible, write a paragraph of ten sentences in which you describe the activities in which you usually participate on any given day. |

_____

_____

_____

_____

_____

_____

_____

EXERCISE O   **Un día especial**   Using as many of the verbs in this chapter, write a paragraph of ten sentences in which you describe the activities in which you usually participate on a special day, such as a birthday, holiday, family outing, and so on.

CHAPTER 3
Interrogatives

1. Question Formation

a. To form a simple question in Spanish (one that anticipates a yes or no response), the subject is usually placed after the verb or at the end of the sentence. In speaking, changing the intonation of the sentence can make the statement into a question (voice rises at the end of the statement).

Uds. viajan mucho.   *You travel a lot.*

¿Uds. viajan mucho?
*¿Viajan **Uds.** mucho?*   ⎫ *Do you travel a lot?*
*¿Viajan **mucho Uds.**?* ⎭

b. Another way to form a question is to add a tag, like *¿no?*, *¿verdad?*, or *¿no es verdad?*, to the end of a sentence. Tag questions can be translated several different ways.

El día es bonito, *¿no?*   *It's a beautiful day, isn't it?*

Mañana celebras tu cumpleaños,   *You celebrate your birthday tomorrow,*
   ¿verdad?   *right? (don't you?)*

EXERCISE A   **Así son.** (That's how they are.)   Jerry is describing a new friend to his mother but she isn't paying close attention to what he says. Express the questions she asks following each of Jerry's comments.

EXAMPLE: Ralph tiene quince años.   **¿Tiene Ralph** quince años?

1. Ralph es alto.

   _____

2. Ralph va a la escuela en bicicleta.

   _____

3. Él hace mucho ejercicio todos los días.

   _____

4. Ralph y su familia pasan las vacaciones de verano en las montañas.

   _____

5. Él es muy inteligente pero divertido.

   _____

6. Ralph y su familia viven en una casa muy grande.

   _____

EXERCISE B | **Pasatiempos** Lisa and a friend are talking about the pastimes of their friends. Lisa likes to verify what she hears by asking a question. Using the tags *¿no?* and *¿verdad?*, express the questions Lisa asks.

EXAMPLE: Ruthie estudia el baile moderno.

Ruthie estudia el baile moderno, **¿verdad?**

1. Gretchen va a correr en el maratón este año.

_____

2. Migdalia toma clases de equitación.

_____

3. Elizabeth pinta paisajes.

_____

4. Lucy y Vicky coleccionan muñecas de otros países.

_____

5. Jane lee varias novelas cada semana.

_____

6. Areli patina en hielo todos los sábados.

_____

2.   Interrogative Expressions

a. Interrogative expressions are used to obtain information.

¿Qué día es hoy?	*What day is today?*
Hoy es martes.	*Today is Tuesday.*
¿Cuántos años tienes?	*How old are you?*
Tengo quince años.	*I am fifteen years old.*

b. Common interrogative expressions

¿qué? *what?*	**¿cuánto(-a)?** *how much?*
¿quién(-es) *who?*	**¿cuántos(-as)?** *how many?*
¿a quién(-es)? *whom?, to whom?*	**¿cómo?** *how?*
¿de quién(-es)? *whose?, of whom?*	**¿por qué?** *why?*
¿con quién(-es)? *with whom?*	**¿dónde?** *where?*
¿cuál(-es)? *which?, which one(s)?*	**¿de dónde?** *(from) where?*
¿cuándo? *when?*	**¿adónde?** *(to) where?*

NOTE: 1.   All interrogative words have a written accent.

2. In Spanish, questions have an inverted question mark (¿) at the beginning and a standard one (?) at the end.

3. When interrogative expressions are used in a question, the subject-verb order is reversed from the order in statements.

¿Qué buscan ellos?	*What are they looking for?*
Ellos buscan pan.	*They are looking for bread.*
¿Cuándo llega Carmen?	*When does Carmen arrive?*
Carmen llega hoy.	*Carmen arrives today.*

c. Uses of the Interrogatives

(1) *¿Qué?* and *¿cuál?* are equivalent to *what?* and *which?*, but the two words are not usually interchangeable in Spanish.

a. *¿Qué?* asks for a description, definition, or explanation.

¿Qué sabor de helado prefieres?	*What flavor ice cream do you prefer?*
¿Qué es un diccionario?	*What is a dictionary?*

b. *¿Cuál?* implies a choice or selection.

¿Cuál de los sabores te gusta más?	*Which flavor do you like more?*

(2) *¿Quién(-es)?*, *¿a quién(-es)*, *¿de quién(-es)*, and *¿con quién(-es)?*

a. *¿Quién(-es)?* (who?) is used as the subject of the sentence.

¿Quién es la señora Vega?	*Who is Mrs. Vega?*
¿Quiénes son esas personas?	*Who are those people?*

b. *¿A quién(-es)?* (whom?, to whom?) is used as the object of the verb (either direct or indirect object).

¿A quién(-es) escribes?	*To whom are you writing?*

c. *¿De quién(-es)?* (whose?) is used to express possession.

¿De quién es la llave?	*Whose key is it?*
¿De quién (-es) son las llaves?	*Whose keys are they?*

NOTE: When prepositions are used with *quién*, the preposition always precedes *quién*.

¿A quién ves todos los días?	*Whom do you see every day?*
¿Con quiénes vas al cine?	*With whom are you going to the movies?*
¿Para quién es el regalo?	*For whom is the gift?*

(3) *¿Dónde?*, *¿adónde?*, and *¿de dónde?*

a. *¿Dónde?* (where?) expresses location.

¿Dónde estás tú?	*Where are you?*

b. *¿Adónde?* (to where?) expresses motion to a place.

¿Adónde van los niños?   *Where are the children going?*

c. *¿De dónde?* (from where?) expresses origin.

¿De dónde es el señor?   *Where is the man from?*

(4) *¿Cómo?*

a. *¿Cómo?*, when used by itself, usually asks for a repetition of something the listener did not hear or understand, or it indicates surprise at what the listener heard.

Jack y Silvia van a casarse.   *Jack and Sylvia are getting married.*
  ¿Cómo?   *—What?*

b. When used with *ser* or *estar*, *¿cómo?* has different meanings.

¿Cómo es tu hermana?   *What is your sister like?*
                            (What does your sister look like?)

¿Cómo está tu hermana?   *How is your sister? (health)*

EXERCISE C   **Muchas preguntas**   Express the questions you asked a new friend to get the information contained in the answers below.

1. Yo me llamo Joe Gines.

   _____

2. Tengo dieciséis años.

   _____

3. Mis padres son de España.

   _____

4. Tengo dos hermanas.

   _____

5. Vivimos en la Avenida Providencia.

   _____

6. Nuestra casa es muy amplia.

   _____

7. Mi profesor de matemáticas es el señor Robles.

   _____

8. Yo voy al gimnasio después de las clases.

   _____

9. Prefiero el fútbol y la natación.

   _____

10. Voy al gimnasio porque me gusta nadar en la piscina.

     _____

11. Mis hermanas y yo ayudamos a nuestros padres.

     _____

12. La mochila es de mi hermana.

     _____

EXERCISE D   **¿Qué o Cuál?**   Indicate which interrogative word is needed in each question.

1. ¿(*Cuál / Qué*) es tu dirección?

2. ¿(*Cuál / Qué*) deportes te gusta practicar?

3. ¿(*Cuál / Qué*) vas a hacer más tarde?

4. ¿(*Cuál / Qué*) de estos refrescos prefieres?

5. ¿(*Cuál / Qué*) clase de comida te gusta más?

6. ¿(*Cuál / Qué*) libro lees ahora?

7. ¿(*Cuáles / Qué*) son los mejores días de la semana?

EXERCISE E   **Preguntas y más preguntas**   Jenny arrives late for a meeting of the Spanish Club at which they are planning an end-of-year celebration. Complete the questions Jenny asks with the appropriate interrogative word.

EXAMPLE: **¿Quién** pone los adornos?

1. ¿ _____ es el mejor día para la fiesta?

2. ¿ _____ deben comprar los refrescos?

3. ¿ _____ van para comprar los refrescos?

4. ¿ _____ invitaciones van a mandar?

5. ¿ _____ tiene lugar la fiesta?

6. ¿ _____ van a adornar el salón?

7. ¿ _____ cuesta asistir a la fiesta?

8. ¿ _____ no piensan invitar a los profesores?

9. ¿ _____ clase de música van a tocar?

10. ¿ _____ van a servir de comer?

11. ¿ _____ debemos pedir permiso?

12. ¿ _____ es el tocadiscos?

EXERCISE F   ¿Cómo? Hay mucho ruido. (What? There's a lot of noise.) You are at a school function with a friend. It's very noisy and you can only hear the answers he gives to another friend's questions. Express the questions based on the information underlined in the responses.

EXAMPLE: Invito a Linda al baile de fin de año.
       ¿A quién invitas al baile de fin de año?

1. Mi familia y yo vamos a pasar las vacaciones en la playa.

   _____

2. Al volver de la playa, trabajo en la oficina de mi papá.

   _____

3. Voy a ahorrar el dinero que gano.

   _____

4. Quiero comprar un carro con el dinero.

   _____

5. Voy a trabajar cinco días a la semana.

   _____

6. Empiezo a trabajar a las ocho y media de la mañana.

   _____

7. Salgo con mis amigos los fines de semana.

   _____

8. Descanso el sábado y el domingo.

   _____

EXERCISE G   La elección   A reporter for the school newspaper is interviewing a student about the upcoming student-government election. Based on the answers provided, express the reporter's questions.

PARA EXPRESARSE MEJOR
Las elecciones estudiantiles   *Student elections*

las elecciones *election*	**prometer** *to promise*
candidato(-ata) *candidate*	**presidente(-enta)** *president*
el oficio *office, position*	**vicepresidente(-enta)** *vice-president*
votar *to vote*	**secretario(-a)** *secretary*
apoyar *to support*	**tesorero(-era)** *treasurer*
la promesa *promise*	**ganar** *to win*
el gobierno estudiantil *student government*	

1. El día de las elecciones es el primero de junio.

   _____

2. Hay dos candidatos para cada oficio.

   _____

3. Todos los estudiantes votan.

   _____

4. Yo apoyo a los candidatos favoritos.

   _____

5. Todos los candidatos hacen muchas promesas.

   _____

6. Prometen una vida mejor en la escuela.

   _____

7. El presidente es el oficio más importante.

   _____

8. Los mejores candidatos van a ganar.

   _____

| EXERCISE H | **Anfitriones** (Hosts)   You and your family will be hosting an exchange student from a Spanish-speaking country during the next school year. Prepare ten questions you will ask him/her to get information about his/her background, interests, plans, goals, and so on. |

1. _____

2. _____

3. _____

4. _____

5. _____

6. _____

7. _____

8. _____

9. _____

10. _____

CHAPTER 4
Verbs with Stem-Changes in the Present Tense

1. Verbs with Stem Changes: *o* to *UE*

a. Many verbs that contain *o* in the stem change the *o* to *ue* in all present tense forms, except for *nosotros* and *vosotros*. (The stem is what is left after you remove the infinitive ending *-ar, -er,* or *-ir.*)

b. This change occurs in the syllable immediately before the verb ending.

c. These verbs have regular endings in the present tense.

	contar *to count*	**poder** *to be able, can, may*	**dormir** *to sleep*
yo	cuento	puedo	duermo
tú	cuentas	puedes	duermes
Ud., él, ella	cuenta	puede	duerme
nosotros, -as	contamos	podemos	dormimos
vosotros, -as	contáis	podéis	dormís
Uds., ellos, ellas	cuentan	pueden	duermen

NOTE: The verb *jugar* (to play) follows the same pattern. The stem vowel changes in all present tense forms except those for *nosotros* and *vosotros: juego, juegas, juega, jugamos, jugáis, juegan.*

Other verbs with stem changes *o* to *ue* are:

almorzar *to eat lunch*   **mostrar** *to show*

costar *to cost*   **recordar** *to remember*

devolver *to return, give back*   **volar** *to fly*

encontrar *to find, to meet*   **volver** *to return, come (go) back*

morir *to die*

EXERCISE A   **Todo el mundo vuela.** Jaime is at the airport awaiting the departure of his flight. Tell where each of the following people are flying to.

EXAMPLE: Jaime / Cancún   Jaime **vuela a** Cancún.

1. Sofía / Buenos Aires   _____

2. Gary y Ben / Londres   _____

3. tú / Atenas   _____

4. Nick y yo / Miami   _____

5. Uds. / San Francisco   _____

6. yo / Barcelona _____

7. el Sr. Pérez / San Juan _____

EXERCISE B   **Devoluciones** (Returns) Genaro is working in the customer service department of a department store. Using the verb *devolver*, tell what items these people return.

EXAMPLE: la señorita / una plancha   La señorita **devuelve** una plancha.

1. el señor / dos corbatas _____

2. tú / un juego electrónico _____

3. Fabio / un traje de baño _____

4. yo / una cadena de oro _____

5. las niñas / dos muñecas _____

6. Kim y Luis / una lámpara _____

EXERCISE C   **Muchas horas de sueño** Tell how many hours these people sleep.

EXAMPLE: mi abuelo / 3 horas   Mi abuelo **duerme tres** horas.

1. yo / 8 horas _____

2. el bebé / 16 horas _____

3. los jóvenes / 12 horas _____

4. mi hermano y yo / 6 horas _____

5. Alfredo / 10 horas _____

6. tú / 5 horas _____

EXERCISE D   **Los deportes favoritos** Tell what sport each of the following people plays.

EXAMPLE: el señor Campos / golf   El señor Campos **juega al** golf.

1. Raquel y Sara / voleibol _____

2. yo / béisbol _____

3. Bill / fútbol _____

4. Vilma y yo / billar _____

5. Justino / boliche _____

6. tú / fútbol americano _____

7. Uds. / baloncesto _____

EXERCISE E **Todos están ocupados.** (Everyone is busy.)   Everyone has a busy schedule today. Tell what these people do.

EXAMPLE: el señor / contar el dinero   El señor **cuenta** el dinero.

1. yo / devolver los regalos

———————————————————————————————————

2. el piloto / volar a Santiago de Chile

———————————————————————————————————

3. mi papá / volver a la oficina

———————————————————————————————————

4. las amigas / almorzar en un restaurante

———————————————————————————————————

5. Valerie y yo / encontrar a los amigos

———————————————————————————————————

6. tú / dormir la siesta

———————————————————————————————————

7. nosotros / contar las invitaciones

———————————————————————————————————

EXERCISE F **Muchas preguntas**   Answer the questions a new friend asks you according to the cues in parentheses.

1. ¿Recuerdas el nombre de tu primera maestra?   (*sí*)

———————————————————————————————————

2. ¿Cuántas horas duermes cada noche?   (*8 horas*)

———————————————————————————————————

3. ¿Dónde almuerzan tú y tus amigos en la escuela?   (*la cafetería*)

———————————————————————————————————

4. ¿Vuela tu familia en avión durante las vacaciones?   (*sí*)

———————————————————————————————————

5. ¿Devuelves los libros a la biblioteca a tiempo?   (*a veces*)

———————————————————————————————————

6. ¿Vuelven Uds. a la escuela después de las clases?   (*no*)

———————————————————————————————————

7. ¿Puedes ir al partido de fútbol el sábado?   (*sí*)

———————————————————————————————————

8. ¿Muestras tus trofeos a tus amigos?   (*sí*)

_____

9. ¿Cuentan los alumnos los días hasta las próximas vacaciones?   (*sí*)

_____

10. ¿Cuánto cuesta la entrada al cine?   (*7 dólares*)

_____

2.   Verbs with Stem Changes: *E* to *IE*

a. Many verbs that contain *e* in the stem change the *e* to *ie* in all present tense forms, except for *nosotros* and *vosotros*. (The stem is what is left after you remove the infinitive ending *-ar, -er,* or *-ir.*)

b. This change occurs in the syllable immediately before the verb ending.

c. These verbs have regular endings in the present tense.

	pensar *to think, to intend*	entender *to understand*	preferir *to prefer*
yo	pienso	entiendo	prefiero
tú	piensas	entiendes	prefieres
Ud., él, ella	piensa	entiende	prefiere
nosotros, -as	pensamos	entendemos	preferimos
vosotros, -as	pensáis	entendéis	preferís
Uds., ellos, ellas	piensan	entienden	prefieren

Other verbs with stem changes *e* to *ie* are:

cerrar *to close*   **perder** *to lose; to waste; to miss (bus, train)*
comenzar *to begin*   **querer** *to want; to wish; to love*
defender *to defend*   **referir** *to tell; to narrate*
empezar *to begin*   **sentir** *to regret, be sorry; to feel*

EXERCISE G   **Planes** Tell what these people intend to do today. Use the verb *pensar* in each statement.

EXAMPLE: Jorge / ver el desfile   Jorge **piensa** ver el desfile.

1. mi abuela / preparar una comida especial

_____

2. tú / asistir a un concierto

_____

3. mis amigos / ir a la piscina

_____

4. yo / leer una novela

_____

5. José Luis y yo / ver una película

_____

6. Gina / encontrar a sus amigas en el centro comercial

_____

7. Laura y Felipe / remar en el lago

_____

| EXERCISE H | **El horario de televisión**   Tell at what time these TV programs begin. Alternate your use of _comenzar_ and _empezar_ in your answers. |

PARA EXPRESARSE MEJOR
El horario de televisión   _Television schedule_

la telenovela _soap opera_   **los concursos** _contests, game shows_

el noticiero _news broadcast_   **de la mañana** _AM_

los documentales _documentaries_   **de la tarde** _PM (afternoon)_

los dibujos animados _cartoons_   **de la noche** _PM_

el pronóstico del tiempo _weather forecast_

EXAMPLE: la película / 7:10 PM
La película **comienza (empieza)** a las siete y diez de la noche.

1. la telenovela / 2:00 PM

_____

2. el primer noticiero del día / 5:00 AM

_____

3. el partido de fútbol / 1:00 PM

_____

4. los documentales / 9:00 AM

_____

5. los dibujos animados / 10:30 AM

_____

6. el pronóstico del tiempo / 6:30 AM

_____

7. los concursos / 8:00 PM

_____

EXERCISE I   **Pérdidas** (Losses) Tell what these people often lose or miss.

EXAMPLE: mi abuelo / los anteojos   Mi abuelo **pierde** los anteojos.

1. Gabriel / las llaves   _____

2. los niños / los juguetes   _____

3. Carlos y yo / el autobús escolar   _____

4. Sally / el anillo   _____

5. tú / el partido de tenis   _____

6. yo / mi programa favorito   _____

7. Amanda y Emma / los aretes   _____

8. Uds. / el tren a la ciudad   _____

EXERCISE J   **Más preguntas** Answer your friend's questions.

1. ¿Prefieres las telenovelas o los concursos?

_____

2. ¿Refieren tus padres muchos cuentos de tu niñez?

_____

3. ¿Piensan tú y tu hermano ir a la playa mañana?

_____

4. ¿Quieres ir conmigo al cine?

_____

5. ¿Empiezan los alumnos a hablar español con el alumno de Costa Rica?

_____

6. ¿Cierras las ventanas de tu cuarto cuando llueve?

_____

7. ¿Defiendes a tu hermano menor?

_____

8. ¿Entienden Uds. los programas de televisión en español?

_____

9. ¿Sienten Uds. no poder ir a la fiesta de Oscar?

_____

10. ¿Comienza el partido a tiempo?

_____

3.   Verbs with Stem Changes: *E* to *I*

a. Only a few *-ir* verbs that contain an *e* in the stem change the *e* to *i* in all present tense forms, except for *nosotros* and *vosotros*. (The stem is what is left after you remove the infinitive ending *-ar*, *-er*, or *-ir*.)

b. This change occurs in the syllable immediately before the verb ending.

c. These verbs have regular endings in the present tense.

repetir *to repeat*			
yo	repito	nosotros, -as	repetimos
tú	repites	vosotros, -as	repetís
Ud., él, ella	repite	Uds., ellos, ellas	repiten

Other verbs with stem changes *e* to *i* are:

medir *to measure*   **reñir** *to quarrel; to scold*

pedir *to ask for, request; to order (food)*   **servir** *to serve*

EXERCISE K   **Me toca a mí.** (It's my turn.)   Tell who asks for the following items on a trip to the amusement park.

EXAMPLE: mi padre / las entradas   Mi padre **pide** las entradas.

1. yo / los refrescos

   _____

2. mi hermano menor / ayuda

   _____

3. Connie y Leticia / el precio de las camisetas

   _____

4. tú / el helado

   _____

5. las niñas / globos

   _____

6. Uds. / permiso para subir al carrusel

   _____

7. mi mamá / un taxi

   _____

EXERCISE L   **¡Qué comida más buena!** (What a delicious meal!)   Your mother receives rave reviews on the food she prepared for a special dinner. Tell who has second servings.

EXAMPLE: mi hermana / la sopa de verduras   Mi hermana **repite** la sopa de verduras.

1. yo / la carne asada   _____

2. mis primos / el postre   _____

3. mi tío / el arroz   _____

4. tú / la salsa   _____

5. mi tía y yo / la ensalada   _____

6. Uds. / las legumbres   _____

| EXERCISE M | **Unas preguntas más**   Answer the questions your grandmother asks about school. |

1. ¿Les riñe la maestra a los alumnos con frecuencia?

   _____

2. ¿Piden los alumnos ayuda cuando la necesitan?

   _____

3. ¿Repites las palabras en la clase de español?

   _____

4. ¿Sirve un alumno de modelo en tu clase?

   _____

5. ¿Miden los profesores el progreso de los alumnos?

   _____

| EXERCISE N | **Reacciones.**   For each statement, give the reaction suggested in parentheses. |

EXAMPLE: Frances tiene mucho sueño. (*dormir la siesta*)   Frances **duerme la siesta.**

1. Debo ir a España este mes. (*volar en avión*)

   _____

2. El niño no obedece a su madre. (*reñirle al niño*)

   _____

3. Beatriz encuentra una cartera en la calle. (*contar el dinero*)

   _____

4. A Pedro le gusta mucho el flan. (*repetir el flan*)

   _____

5. Vicente es muy deportista. (*jugar al fútbol y al béisbol*)

   _____

6. Yo no entiendo el problema de matemáticas. (*pedir ayuda*)

   _____

7. Mi mamá va a comprar una alfombra para la sala.   (*medir la sala*)

   _____

8. Nos gusta viajar.   (*pensar viajar a Venezuela*)

   _____

9. El cielo está muy nublado.   (*comenzar a llover*)

   _____

10. John y Terry quieren comprar más camisetas.   (*volver a la tienda mañana*)

   _____

| EXERCISE O | **Feliz viaje.**   The family depicted in the following drawing is leaving on a trip. Using as many of the stem-changing in this chapter, write a story of then sentences in which you describe their trip, what they intend to do during the flight and when they get to their destination, and so on. |

   _____

   _____

   _____

   _____

   _____

   _____

   _____

   _____

   _____

CHAPTER 5

SER; Expressing Possession with *DE*; Nouns and Articles; *HAY*

In Spanish there are two different verbs, *ser* and *estar*, that correspond to the English verb *to be*. The use of each verb depends on the context.

1. *SER*

    a. The forms of *ser* are irregular.

ser *to be*			
yo	soy	nosotros, -as	somos
tú	eres	vosotros, -as	sois
Ud., él, ella	es	Uds., ellos, ellas	son

    b. *Ser* expresses a characteristic, description, or identification.

        (1) Characteristics

            La mujer *es bondadosa.*   *The woman is kind.*

            El acero *es duro.*   *Steel is hard.*

        (2) Description

            Jerry *es fuerte.*   *Jerry is strong.*

            La casa *es amplia.*   *The house is ample (large).*

        (3) Identification

            ¿Quién es?   *Who is it?*

            Es Miguel.   *It's Miguel.*

    c. *Ser* expresses an occupation or nationality.

        (1) Occupation

            Mi madre *es dentista.*   *My mother is a dentist.*

            Ellas *son programadoras.*   *They are programmers.*

        (2) Nationality

            Yo *soy costarricense.*   *I am Costa Rican.*

            Mis abuelos *son italianos.*   *My grandparents are Italian.*

    d. *Ser* expresses dates and time.

        (1) Dates

            Es el primero de octubre.   *It's October 1.*

            Es el veinte de enero.   *It's January 20.*

(2) Time

Son las once.	*It's eleven o'clock.*
Es mediodía.	*It's noon.*

e. *Ser* + *de* expresses origin or material.

(1) Origin

¿De dónde es **el actor?**	*Where is the actor from?*
El actor *es de España.*	*The actor is from Spain.*

(2) Material

¿De qué es **el libro?**	*What is the book made of?*
El libro *es de papel.*	*The book is made of paper.*

NOTE: 1.   Adjectives used with ser must agree with the subject in number and gender.

Luis y Felipe *son* **delgados.**	*Luis and Felipe are thin.*
Sonia *es* **delgada también.**	*Sonia is thin too.*

2.   In questions, the adjective usually follows the verb.

¿Son antiguas **las ruinas?**	*Are the ruins ancient?*

3.   The adjective *feliz* is usually used with *ser*.

El niño *es feliz.*	*The boy is happy.*

EXERCISE A   **Así son mis amigos.** (My friends are like this.) Johnny is talking about himself and his friends. Tell what he says using the adjectives provided.

EXAMPLE: Lisa / simpático   Lisa es **simpática.**

1. Rodolfo / divertido   _____

2. Clara e Inés / responsable   _____

3. tú y Peter / generoso   _____

4. yo / independiente   _____

5. Mari / bondadoso   _____

6. Kyoto y yo / amable   _____

7. tú / tacaño   _____

8. todos mis amigos / simpático _____

EXERCISE B   **Nacionalidades** Kurt is talking with some foreign students and one of his friends joins the group. Introduce each one and tell their nationality.

EXAMPLE: Kim / Corea   Kim **es de** Corea. Ella **es coreana.**

1. Giuseppe / Italia _____

2. Antonio y Rafael / Argentina _____

3. Belinda / México _____

4. yo / Alemania _____

5. Sarita y Juan Carlos / España _____

6. Elisabeth y yo / Alemania _____

7. Migdalia / Venezuela _____

8. Rebecca y Amanda / Puerto Rico _____

EXERCISE C   **¡Estoy orgulloso / orgullosa!** (I'm proud.)   Sam is talking about what people he knows do for a living. Express what he says.

> ### PARA EXPRESARSE MEJOR
> #### Las profesiones *Professions*
>
> | | |
> |---|---|
> | **médico(-a)** *doctor* | **ingeniero(-era)** *engineer* |
> | **mecánico(-a)** *mechanic* | **locutor(-ora)** *announcer* |
> | **arquitecto(-a)** *architect* | **bombero(-era)** *fireman* |
> | **estudiante** (m. & f.) *student* | **abogado(-ada)** *lawyer* |

EXAMPLE: Mi abuela enseña en una escuela primaria.   Mi abuela es **profesora (maestra)**.

1. Mi papá defiende a las personas en la corte.

   _____

2. Mi mamá cura a los enfermos.

   _____

3. Vicente diseña casas y edificios nuevos.

   _____

4. Sally repara motores.

   _____

5. Tú construyes edificios altos y puentes.

   _____

6. Los hermanos de Pablo apagan los incendios.

   _____

7. Sandra quiere anunciar los programas en la televisión.

   _____

8. Jenny y yo asistimos a la escuela.

   _____

EXERCISE D | **¿Qué día es?** (What day is it?)   Based on this excerpt from Les's calendar tell what day and date he is in the places indicated.

AUGUST						
SUNDAY	MONDAY	TUESDAY	WEDNESDAY	THURSDAY	FRIDAY	SATURDAY
6	7	8	9	10	11	12
Atlanta	Madrid	Toledo	Segovia	Burgos	Sevilla	Granada

EXAMPLE: Segovia   **Es miércoles, el nueve de agosto.**

1. Granada _____

2. Atlanta _____

3. Sevilla _____

4. Madrid _____

5. Burgos _____

6. Toledo _____

EXERCISE E | **De compras** (Shopping)   Jessie isn't doing well on a shopping trip because she doesn't like the materials the items are made of. Tell what the items she looked at are made of.

EXAMPLE: las sandalias / plástico   Las sandalias **son de** plástico.

1. el vestido / seda   _____

2. el reloj / oro   _____

3. la bolsa / cuero   _____

4. los pantalones / algodón   _____

5. el traje de baño / lana   _____

6. los aretes / plata   _____

EXERCISE F | **Una llamada telefónica** (A telephone call)   You call a new friend's house, and his younger sister answers. Answer her questions.

1. Hola. ¿Quién es?

   TÚ: _____

2. ¿De dónde eres?

   TÚ: _____

3. ¿Cómo eres?

   TÚ: _____

4. ¿Cuál es tu profesión?

   TÚ: _____

5. ¿Qué día es hoy?

   TÚ: _____

6. ¿De qué es el teléfono?

   TÚ: _____

7. ¿Qué hora es?

   TÚ: _____

2.   Expressing Possession with *DE*

Ser + de is used to express possession.

¿*De* quién *es* la computadora?	*Whose computer is it?*
La computadora *es de* mi tío.	*It's my uncle's computer.*
La computadora *es de* Jack.	*It's Jack's computer.*
La computadora *es del* profesor.	*It's the teacher's computer.*

NOTE: 1.   When *de* is followed by *el*, the contraction *del* is formed.

La casa es del señor Galas.	*It's Mr. Galas' house.*
El trineo es del muchacho.	*It's the boy's sled.*

2.   When *de* is followed by the *la, los,* or *las*, no change takes place.

El reloj *es de la* señora.	*It's the woman's watch.*
Los lápices *son de los* alumnos.	*They are the students' pencils.*
Las muñecas *son de las* niñas.	*They are the girls' dolls.*

EXERCISE G   **Posesiones**   After a school trip, the bus driver returns items that were left behind on the bus by the students. Tell to whom the items belong.

EXAMPLE: la cámara / Brian   La cámara **es de** Brian.

1. las mochilas / Ricardo y Ana   _____

2. los anteojos de sol / Carolina   _____

3. el suéter / Natalie   _____

4. las llaves / la señora Castilla   _____

5. los tenis / Enrique   _____

6. el anillo / Manny   _____

EXERCISE H   ¿**De quién es?**   After the party in Juan's house ends, he returns items to their owners. For each item, express Juan's question and the response, according to the cues provided.

EXAMPLE: el tocadiscos / Enrique
        ¿**De quién es el tocadiscos?**
        Es de Enrique.

1. los discos / Susana y Elvira

   _____

   _____

2. las velas / Marisol

   _____

   _____

3. la guitarra / Pedro

   _____

   _____

4. las maracas / Álvaro

   _____

   _____

5. el radio portátil / Gustavo

   _____

   _____

6. los juegos electrónicos / Esteban y Nilda

   _____

   _____

EXERCISE I   **Amigo por correspondencia** (Pen pal)   Write a note of six sentences in Spanish to a new pen pal. Introduce yourself; tell where you are from, your nationality, and describe your physical and personality characteristics.

_____

_____

_____

_____

_____

_____

3.   Nouns and Articles

Nouns refer to people, animals, places, and things. All nouns in Spanish are either masculine or feminine.

a. Nouns ending in *-o* and nouns referring to male beings are generally masculine.

el abuelo	*grandfather*	**el hombre**	*man*
el amigo	*friend*	**el padre**	*father*
el cuaderno	*notebook*	**el profesor**	*teacher*
el disco	*record*	**el señor**	*man*

b. Nouns ending in *-a, -d,* or *-ión* and nouns referring to female beings are generally feminine.

la abuela	*grandmother*	**la madre**	*mother*
la actividad	*activity*	**la mujer**	*woman*
la escuela	*school*	**la nacionalidad**	*nationality*
la lección	*lesson*	**la niña**	*girl*

c. Some nouns are either masculine or feminine.

el / la adolescente	*teenager*	**el / la joven**	*young man / woman*
el / la estudiante	*student*		

d. Some nouns ending in *-a* are masculine and some nouns ending in *-o* are feminine.

MASCULINE	FEMININE
el clima *climate*	**la foto(grafía)** *photo(graph)*
el día *day*	**la mano** *hand*
el idioma *language*	**la radio** *radio*

e. The gender of other nouns must be learned individually.

el árbol	*tree*	**la flor**	*flower*
el lápiz	*pencil*	**la noche**	*night*
el papel	*paper*	**la sal**	*salt*
el pie	*foot*	**la tarde**	*afternoon*

f. The articles used before masculine singular nouns are *el* (the) and *un* (a, an). The articles used before feminine singular nouns are *la* (the) and *una* (a, an).

MASCULINE	FEMININE
el hermano *the brother*	**la hermana** *the sister*
un museo *a museum*	**una biblioteca** *a library*

g. In a series of nouns, the article is generally repeated before each noun.

Busco *un* chaleco y *una* corbata.	*I'm looking for a vest and a tie.*
Compro *el* pan y *la* leche.	*I buy the bread and the milk.*

EXERCISE J   **De compras**   Express the definite article (*el* or *la*) for the items Lucy found on her shopping list.

EXAMPLE: ___**el**___ pescado

1. _____ pan

2. _____ helado

3. _____ mantequilla

4. _____ mermelada

5. _____ fruta

6. _____ leche

7. _____ carne

8. _____ cereal

9. _____ lechuga

10. _____ sal

EXERCISE K   **Analogías** (Analogies)   In each group, express the missing word with its corresponding definite article (*el* or *la*).

EXAMPLE: el sobrino : la sobrina : el hijo : ___**la hija**___

1. el abuelo : la abuela : _____ : la madre

2. el doctor : la doctora : el paciente : _____

3. _____ : la pluma : la pizarra : la tiza

4. el anillo : el dedo : la corbata : _____

5. el pantalón : la falda : la camisa : _____

6. el dinero : el banco : _____ : el estómago

7. _____ : el pie : el guante : la mano

8. el juguete : el niño : la computadora : _____

9. el mes : _____ : el capítulo : el libro

10. el guía : el viaje : _____ : el avión

h. Nouns ending in a vowel form the plural by adding *-s*.

SINGULAR	PLURAL
el bolígrafo	los bolígrafos
la goma	las gomas
un juguete	unos juguetes
una madre	unas madres

i. Nouns ending in a consonant form the plural by adding *-es*.

SINGULAR	PLURAL
el doctor	los doctores
la actividad	las actividades

j. Nouns ending in *-z* change *z* to *c* before adding *-es*.

SINGULAR	PLURAL
el lápiz	los lápices
la voz	las voces

k. An accent mark is added or dropped in nouns ending in *n* or *s* to keep the original stress.

SINGULAR	PLURAL
el joven	los jóvenes
el examen	los exámenes
el francés	los franceses
la acción	las acciones

NOTE: 1. The plural of *el* and *la* is *los* and *las*, respectively.

2. The plural of *un* and *una* is *unos* and *unas*, respectively. *Unos / unas* mean *some, a few,* or *several*.

EXERCISE L **Yo veo más cosas.** During a visit to the zoo, Jimmy claims he sees more things than his friend Pepe. Based on what Pepe says, express Jimmy's comment.

EXAMPLE: Yo veo el (un) elefante.   Yo veo **los (unos)** elefantes.

1. Yo veo la jirafa. _____

2. Yo veo el león. _____

3. Yo veo el pájaro. _____

4. Yo veo la serpiente. _____

5. Yo veo el puma. _____

6. Yo veo el rinoceronte.   _____

7. Yo veo la cebra.   _____

EXERCISE M   **La barbacoa** (The cookout)   You are helping your mother prepare the table for a cookout. Express what she says she needs.

EXAMPLE: plato   Necesito **unos platos.**

1. tenedor   _____

2. vaso   _____

3. servilleta   _____

4. cuchillo   _____

5. mantel   _____

6. flor   _____

l.   There are four definite articles in Spanish that correspond to English *the*.

	SINGULAR	PLURAL
MASCULINE	el	los
FEMININE	la	las

NOTE: Feminine nouns that begin with a stressed *a* sound (*a-* or *ha-*) take the articles *el* and *un* in the singular. In the plural, they take *las* and *unas*.

SINGULAR		PLURAL	
el agua un agua	water	las aguas unas aguas	waters
el aula un aula	classroom	las aulas unas aulas	classrooms
el hacha un hacha	ax	las hachas unas hachas	axes

m.   There are four indefinite articles in Spanish that correspond to English *a* (*an*), *some*, *a few*, and *several*.

	SINGULAR	PLURAL
MASCULINE	un	unos
FEMININE	una	unas

un primo   *a cousin*   **unos primos**   *some cousins*
una camisa   *a shirt*   **unas camisas**   *a few shirts*

n. The definite article is used:

    (1) before the names of languages, unless the language follows *hablar, en* or *de.*

El español es muy popular.	*Spanish is very popular.*
Estudio el francés.	*I study French.*

    BUT:

Ella habla italiano.	*She speaks Italian.*
Escriben en árabe.	*They write in Arabic.*
Mi clase de español es divertida.	*My Spanish class is entertaining.*

    (2) before titles, except when speaking directly to a person.

La señora Pardo habla mucho.	*Mrs. Pardo talks a lot.*
El doctor Ruiz llama ahora.	*Dr. Ruiz is calling now.*

    BUT:

Señor Alba, ¿cómo está Ud.?	*How are you, Mr. Alba?*

    (3) before the nouns *escuela, clase,* and *iglesia,* when they follow a preposition.

Vamos a *la* escuela.	*We are going to school.*
Mi mamá está en *la* iglesia.	*My mother is in church.*

    (4) before the days of the week, to express the English preposition *on.*

Mi papá no trabaja *los* sábados.	*My father doesn't work on Saturdays.*

    BUT:

Hoy es jueves.	*Today is Thursday.*

o. The indefinite article is used to express English *a (an).*

Tienen *un* hermano y *una* hermana.	*They have a brother and a sister.*

p. When adjectives expressing nationality or nouns expressing professions or occupations follow *ser,* the indefinite article is omitted. If the adjective or noun is modified, the indefinite article is used.

Sara *es* española.	*Sara is Spanish.*
Mi abuelo *es* abogado.	*My grandfather is a lawyer.*
Ella quiere *ser* locutora.	*She wants to be an announcer.*

    BUT:

Mi abuelo *es un* abogado bueno.	*My grandfather is a good lawyer.*

EXERCISE N   **Un día especial** (A special day)   Raymond wrote the following letter while traveling with his parents in Spain. Complete the letter using the appropriate definite or indefinite article, as needed.

Hoy ——————— señor Dávila va a comer y pasar ——————— tarde con nosotros.
       1.   2.

Él es ——————— antiguo amigo de mi papá. Ellos son ——————— amigos
          3.   4.

desde sus días en ——————— universidad. ——————— señor Dávila habla
                        5.   6.

——————— inglés, ——————— español y ——————— japonés. Él vive
     6.   7.   8.

en ——————— suburbios de Madrid y es ——————— guía turístico.
      10.   11.

Después de ——————— comida, nosotros vamos a visitar ———————
                12.   13.

Museo del Prado porque hay ——————— estreno de ——————— exposición
                                14.   15.

especial. ——————— señor Dávila es ——————— especialista en ———————
              16.   17.   18.

arte del siglo XIX. A mí me gustan ——————— pinturas de este siglo. Prefiero
                                         19.

——————— retratos de ——————— Familia Real. Ahora me despido.
      20.   21.

Es ——————— hora de ——————— comida. Hasta ——————— vista.
      22.   23.   24.

Raymond

4.   *HAY*

a. *Hay* expresses English *there is* and *there are*. Its form remains the same before both singular and plural nouns. As a question, *¿hay?* means *is there?* or *are there?*

Hay un plato limpio en la mesa.	*There is a clean plate on the table.*
Hay platos limpios en la cocina.	*There are clean plates in the kitchen.*
¿Hay platos limpios en la mesa?	*Are there clean plates on the table?*

b. To express *how many?*, *¿cuántos hay?* (*¿cuántas hay?*) is used.

¿Cuántos periódicos hay?	*How many newspapers are there?*
¿Cúantas sillas hay?	*How many chairs are there?*

EXERCISE O   **¿Cuántos hay?** Larry is playing a game with his younger brother. Using the cues provided, tell how his brother answers the questions.

EXAMPLE: ¿Cuántos carros hay en la calle? (*muchos*)   Hay **muchos** carros en la calle.

1. ¿Cuántos dedos hay en cada mano? (*5*)

   _____

2. ¿Cuántas estrellas hay en el cielo? (*muchas*)

   _____

3. ¿Cuántas personas hay en la tienda? (*20*)

_____

4. ¿Cuántas familias hay en esta cuadra? (*18*)

_____

5. ¿Cuántos juguetes hay en la tienda? (*1,000*)

_____

6. ¿Cuántos perros hay en el parque? (*25*)

_____

| EXERCISE P | **¿Qué hay?**   Express what you see in this drawing.

Hay _____

_____

_____

_____

_____

_____

_____

_____ .

CHAPTER 6
ESTAR; The Present Progressive; Uses of *SER* and *ESTAR*

In Spanish there are two different verbs, *ser* and *estar*, that correspond to the English verb *to be*. The use of each verb depends on the context. (The forms and uses of *ser* are explained in Chapter 5.)

1. *ESTAR*

a. Forms of *estar*

estar *to be*			
yo	estoy	nosotros, -as	estamos
tú	estás	vosotros, -as	estáis
Ud., él, ella	está	Uds., ellos, ellas	están

b. Uses of *estar*

(1) To express location or position.

Dallas *está en Tejas.*	*Dallas is (located) in Texas.*
Mi abuelo *está en España.*	*My grandfather is in Spain.*
Los lápices *están en la mesa.*	*The pencils are on the table.*
¿Dónde estás?	*Where are you?*

(2) To express a changing condition or state with an adjective.

El refresco *está frío.*	*The soda is cold.*
Mi tía *está contenta.*	*My aunt is happy.*
¿Cómo estás? —Estoy así así.	*How are you? —I'm so so.*

(3) To express a condition that is the result of an action.

El niño *está acostado.*	*The boy is lying down.*
La tienda *está cerrada.*	*The store is closed.*
Las luces *están apagadas.*	*The lights are out.*

NOTE: 1. Adjectives used with *estar* agree with the subject in number and gender.

Gloria *está preocupada.*	*Gloria is worried.*
Los padres *están preocupados.*	*The parents are worried.*

2. In questions, the adjective usually follows the verb.

¿Está preocupada **Gloria?**	*Is Gloria worried?*
¿Están preocupados **los padres?**	*Are the parents worried?*

EXERCISE A   **Cada cosa en su lugar.** (Everything in its place.) Tony can't find anything after his mother straightened his room. Express Tony's questions and his mother's responses.

EXAMPLE: la mochila / el armario
           ¿Dónde está la mochila?
           Está en el armario.

1. mis libros / el estante

_____

_____

2. el guante de béisbol / el sótano

_____

_____

3. los videojuegos / el escritorio

_____

_____

4. el fútbol / el patio

_____

_____

5. el teléfono portátil / la cocina

_____

_____

6. las tarjetas de béisbol / el álbum

_____

_____

EXERCISE B   **¿Dónde está . . . ?** Grace is spending the summer in a small town and is trying to familiarize herself with the location of different places in town. Using the map below, tell the location of the places indicated.

PARA EXPRESARSE MEJOR
Ubicación *Location*

cerca de *near to*	**frente a** *opposite, facing*
lejos de *far from*	**detrás de** *behind*
al lado de *next to*	**delante de** *in front of*

EXAMPLE: la escuela / el parque   La escuela **está cerca del** parque.

1. el cine / el correo   _____

2. el restaurante / el supermercado   _____

3. el banco / la escuela   _____

4. el cine / el supermercado   _____

5. el banco / la biblioteca   _____

6. la florería / la biblioteca   _____

EXERCISE C   **El partido** (The game)   It's the day of the big school football game. Tell how everyone is.

EXAMPLE: el entrenador / nervioso   El entrenador **está** nervioso.

1. Miguel y Antón / preocupado   _____

2. los aficionados / alegre   _____

3. tú / desilusionado   _____

4. mis amigos y yo / ansioso   _____

5. Esmeralda y Joan / animado   _____

6. yo / contento   _____

7. los padres / orgulloso   _____

| EXERCISE D | ¡Todo está preparado! (Everything is prepared!)   When Jenny arrives at her aunt's house for a special dinner, her aunt tells her what is already prepared. Express what her aunt says. |

EXAMPLE: la mesa / puesto   La mesa **ya está puesta**.

1. la sopa / caliente _____

2. la carne / asado _____

3. el helado / congelado _____

4. las velas / encendido _____

5. las legumbres / limpio _____

6. los regalos / envuelto _____

2.   The Present Progressive

a. The present progressive is used to express an action that is in progress or continuing at the moment indicated. It is formed with the present tense of *estar* and the gerund or *-ing* form (present participle) of the action verb.

b. Regular verbs form the gerund by dropping the infinitive ending and adding *-ando* (*-ar* verbs) and *-iendo* (*-er* and *-ir* verbs) to the stem.

INFINITIVE	GERUND	MEANING
bailar	bailando	dancing
hacer	haciendo	doing, making
escribir	escribiendo	writing

c. Irregular *-er* and *-ir* verbs with stems ending in a vowel form their gerunds by adding *-yendo*.

caer: cayendo *falling*   **leer: leyendo** *reading*
construir: construyendo *constructing*   **oír: oyendo** *hearing*
creer: creyendo *believing*   **traer: trayendo** *bringing*
ir: yendo *going*

d. Stem-changing *-ir* verbs change their stem vowel from *e* to *i* and from *o* to *u* in the gerund.

decir: diciendo *saying, telling*   **pedir: pidiendo** *asking for*
dormir: durmiendo *sleeping*   **sentir: sintiendo** *feeling; regretting*
morir: muriendo *dying*   **venir: viniendo** *coming*

e. The gerund of *poder* is *pudiendo*.

f. When direct-and-indirect object pronouns are used with verbs in the present progressive tense, the pronoun may either precede the form of *estar* or it may be attached to the gerund (present participle). If the pronoun is attached to the gerund, an accent mark is placed over the *a* or *e* of the gerund ending to preserve the original stress: *comprándolo, comiéndolos, diciéndonos.*

¿Me estás hablando?	*Are you talking to me?*
Sí, *te estoy* hablando.	*Yes, I am speaking to you.*
Sí, estoy *hablándote*.	
¿Están Uds. bebiendo leche?	*Are you drinking milk?*
No, no *la estamos* bebiendo.	*No, we are not drinking it.*
No, no estamos *bebiéndola*.	

EXERCISE E   **¿Qué estás haciendo?** (What are you doing?)   As the teacher goes around the room working with individual students or small groups, she wants to know what everyone is doing. Express the students' responses.

EXAMPLE: Mario, ¿qué estás haciendo? (*estudiar*)   Yo **estoy estudiando.**

1. Bruce y Morgan, ¿qué están haciendo Uds.? (*practicar el diálogo*)

   _____

2. Silvia, ¿qué estás haciendo? (*escribir una carta*)

   _____

3. Jackie, ¿qué está haciendo Elias? (*preparar la tarea*)

   _____

4. Mirta, ¿qué están haciendo Rogelio y Hugo? (*comer galletas*)

   _____

5. Allen, ¿qué estoy haciendo yo? (*ayudar a los alumnos*)

   _____

EXERCISE F   **Todos están ocupados.** (Everyone is busy.)   Tell what each member of the Amaya family is doing.

EXAMPLE: el padre / lavar los platos   El padre **está lavando** los platos.

1. la madre / barrer el piso

   _____

2. Jeffrey y Evan / jugar al baloncesto

   _____

3. el señor Amaya / leer el periódico

   _____

4. tú / dormir la siesta

_____

5. el abuelo / decir chistes

_____

6. yo / pedir ayuda

_____

7. nosotros / oír música

_____

EXERCISE G   **Pasatiempos** (Pastimes)   People spend a lot of time at their hobbies. Express what these people are doing right now.

EXAMPLE: Alfonso colecciona monedas.   Alfonso **está coleccionando** monedas.

1. Luz y Adriana esquían en las montañas.

_____

2. Yo practico el tenis.

_____

3. Tú y Enzo juegan al ajedrez.

_____

4. Nosotros asistimos a un concierto.

_____

5. Gilda escribe poesías.

_____

6. Tú sacas fotografías.

_____

7. Emily hace yoga.

_____

8. Mis hermanos corren en el parque.

_____

EXERCISE H   **Preparando la fiesta**   Ruth is keeping her young cousin out of trouble while everyone prepares for her birthday party. Express Ruth's answers when she asks what everyone is doing. Express her response two ways using the present progressive and the appropriate object pronoun.

EXAMPLE: ¿Prepara la abuela el pastel?
          Sí, la abuela **lo está preparando.**
          Sí, la abuela **está preparándolo.**

1. ¿Cuelga mi papá los adornos?

   _____

   _____

2. ¿Arman Gary y Lucy los juegos?

   _____

   _____

3. ¿Infla Carlos los globos?

   _____

   _____

4. ¿Lee Adela mis tarjetas de cumpleaños?

   _____

   _____

5. ¿Escogemos nosotras la música?

   _____

   _____

6. ¿Ponemos los regalos en la mesa?

   _____

   _____

7. ¿Tú me ayudas?

   _____

   _____

| EXERCISE I | **Todos ayudan.** Tell what each person is doing to help at home. Use the present progressive and the appropriate object pronoun. Express the action two ways. |

EXAMPLE: Jack contesta el teléfono.
Jack **lo está contestando.**
Jack **está contestándolo.**

1. La abuela plancha la ropa.

   _____

   _____

2. Gregorio le da de comer al gato.

   _____

   _____

3. Roger y Lina sacuden los muebles.

_____

_____

4. Yo recojo las hojas en el jardín.

_____

_____

5. Alicia me pide otro favor.

_____

_____

6. Tú barres el piso de la cocina.

_____

_____

7. Mi mamá nos ofrece un refresco.

_____

_____

3.   *SER* and *ESTAR*

a. The general uses of *ser* are explained in Chapter 5; those of *estar* are explained earlier in this chapter.

b. Some adjectives may be used with either *ser* or *estar*, but their meanings change.

Pedro *es* pálido.	*Pedro is pale. (Pedro's complexion is pale.)*
Pedro *está* pálido.	*Pedro is pale. (Pedro turned pale.)*
Los hermanos *son* listos.	*The brothers are clever.*
Los hermanos *están* listos.	*The brothers are ready.*
La señora *es* joven.	*The woman is young.*
La señora *está* joven.	*The woman looks young.*

c. Other adjectives that have different meanings when used with *ser* or *estar*

ADJECTIVE	SER	ESTAR
aburrido	*to be boring*	*to be bored*
nervioso	*to be nervous (to be a nervous person)*	*to feel nervous*
seguro	*to be safe, reliable*	*to be sure, certain*
viejo	*to be old*	*to look old*
vivo	*to be quick*	*to be alive*

d. When talking about food, *bueno* and *malo* have different meanings with *ser* or *estar*.

Las verduras *son* buenas.	*The vegetables are good (healthy).*
Las verduras *están* buenas.	*The vegetables taste good.*

EXERCISE J	**Comentarios** (Commentaries) Jean always comments about what she hears. Express her comments using ser or estar with the following adjectives: *aburrido, joven, listo, nervioso, pálido, seguro, viejo, vivo.*

EXAMPLE: Carrie espera el resultado de un examen.   Carrie **está nerviosa.**

1. Los niños corren por toda la casa y gritan mucho.

   _____

2. A Emilio no le gusta el programa de televisión.

   _____

3. La señora Muñoz usa mucho maquillaje en la cara.

   _____

4. Sara siempre resuelve las adivinanzas.

   _____

5. Guillermo contesta todas las preguntas correctamente sin pensar.

   _____

6. Tu abuela usa ropa moderna.

   _____

7. Felipe y Greg están enfermos.

   _____

8. El padre de Vicente trabaja demasiado.

   _____

9. Mi tía tiene veinte años.

   _____

10. Tus padres siempre miran por la ventana cuando tú llegas tarde.

    _____

11. Carolina quiere regresar a su casa ahora mismo.

    _____

12. El profesor de matemáticas no cambia la voz en la clase.

    _____

| EXERCISE K |

Incompleto (Incomplete)   Zach received this electronic message from a new friend but some of the words were missing. Complete the message with the appropriate forms of *ser* or *estar*.

Hola amigo:

Yo ——————— Héctor Ramos. Yo ——————— muy bien hoy. Mi familia y
      1.   2.

yo ——————— en San José. Nosotros ——————— de Costa Rica.
     3.   4.

——————— alto y delgado. Mis amigos dicen: —Héctor, tú ——————— muy
  5.   6.

simpático. Yo ——————— escribiéndote este mensaje mientras ——————— en
       7.   8.

la clase de computación.

Me gusta viajar y cuando mi familia y yo ——————— de vacaciones, visitamos
                9.

otros países. Tengo muchos intereses y raras veces ——————— aburrido. Mi casa
                          10.

——————— en una sección bonita de la ciudad. ——————— una casa grande y
  11.   12.

cómoda. ——————— cerca de la escuela. Yo ——————— listo para hacer
        13.   14.

nuevos amigos. Mis amigos y yo ——————— muy vivos en las fiestas. Escríbeme
              15.

pronto.

Héctor

| EXERCISE L |

De vacaciones (On vacation)   Write a letter of ten sentences in Spanish to a friend. Describe the vacation you are enjoying. Tell where you are, a description of the vacation area, how you feel, and what you are doing while vacationing. Use *ser* or *estar* in your sentences, as needed.

_____

_____

_____

_____

_____

_____

_____

_____

_____

CHAPTER 7
Adjectives; Shortening of Adjectives; Comparisons

1. Adjectives

Adjectives describe nouns and agree in number (singular or plural) and gender (masculine or feminine) with the nouns they modify.

a. Agreement of Adjectives

(1) Adjectives ending in -*o* change -*o* to -*a* when they describe a feminine singular noun.

Juan es delgado.	*Juan is thin.*
Lucy es delgada.	*Lucy is thin.*

(2) Adjectives ending in -*e* or a consonant remain the same when they describe a feminine noun.

El señor es diligente.	*The man is diligent.*
La mujer es diligente.	*The woman is diligent.*
El libro es fácil.	*The book is easy.*
La clase es fácil.	*The class is easy.*

(3) Adjectives of nationality that end in a consonant add an -*a* when they describe a feminine singular noun.

Charles es inglés.	*Charles is English.*
Elizabeth es inglesa.	*Elizabeth is English.*

(4) The plural of adjectives is formed as follows: if the adjective ends in a vowel an -*s* is added; if it ends in a consonant -*es* or -*as* is added.

SINGULAR	PLURAL
Juan es delgado.	Juan y Felipe son delgados.
Lucy es delgada.	Lucy y Ana son delgadas.
El señor es diligente.	Los señores son diligentes.
La mujer es diligente.	Las mujeres son diligentes.
Charles es inglés.	Charles y Brian son ingleses.
Elizabeth es inglesa.	Elizabeth y Jane son inglesas.
El libro es fácil.	Los libros son fáciles.
La clase es fácil.	Las clases son fáciles.

(5) Adjectives that modify two or more nouns of different gender use the masculine plural.

El hombre y la mujer son simpáticos.	*The man and the woman are nice.*
Charles y Elizabeth son ingleses.	*Charles and Elizabeth are English.*

NOTE: 1. Adjectives ending in -*o* have four forms:

bonito, bonita, bonitos, bonitas

2. Adjectives ending in -*e* or a consonant have two forms, one singular and one plural:

inteligente, inteligentes; difícil, difíciles

3. Adjectives of nationality ending in a consonant have four forms:

español, española, españoles, españolas

4. Adjectives of nationality with an accent on the last syllable drop the accent mark in the feminine singular and in both plural forms:

japonés, japonesa, japoneses, japonesas

alemán, alemana, alemanes, alemanas

EXERCISE A **Los colores** Ricky describes what he sees as he looks out the window. Using the cues indicated, tell the color of the things he sees.

> ## PARA EXPRESARSE MEJOR
> ### Los colores
>
> | | | | |
> |---|---|---|---|
> | **amarillo** | *yellow* | **negro** | *black* |
> | **anaranjado** | *orange* | **pardo** | *brown* |
> | **azul** | *blue* | **rojo** | *red* |
> | **blanco** | *white* | **rosado** | *pink* |
> | **gris** | *gray* | **verde** | *green* |
> | **morado** | *purple* | | |

EXAMPLE: la mochila / rojo   La mochila es **roja.**

1. la casa / azul _____

2. la flor / rosado _____

3. el automóvil / negro _____

4. la nube / gris _____

5. el autobús / amarillo _____

6. la estrella / blanco _____

7. la hoja / anaranjado _____

8. el globo / morado _____

9. el árbol / pardo _____

10. la planta / verde _____

EXERCISE B | **¿De qué color son?** Ricky's sister sees more than one of each of the things he identified before. Using Ricky's statements in **Exercise A**, tell what she sees.

EXAMPLE: La mochila es roja.   Las mochilas son **rojas**.

1. _____
2. _____
3. _____
4. _____
5. _____
6. _____
7. _____
8. _____
9. _____
10. _____

EXERCISE C | **¿Cómo son?** (What are they like?)   Janet is describing the people in her class. Express what he says.

EXAMPLE: Victoria / inteligente   Victoria es **inteligente**.

1. Norma / bonito   _____
2. Larry / divertido   _____
3. Jack y Elsa / cómico   _____
4. Mirta / simpático   _____
5. Ralph y Nick / fuerte   _____
6. Carmen / responsable   _____
7. Tomás / descortés   _____
8. la Sra. Ayala / estricto _____

EXERCISE D | **¿Qué nacionalidad?** (What nationality?)   Inés is attending a workshop for exchange students. Express the nationalities of the following students.

EXAMPLE: Inés / ecuatoriano   Inés es **ecuatoriana**.

1. Raúl y Nilda / español   _____

2. Gustavo / portugués   _____

3. Andrea / inglés   _____

4. Laura y Aldo / italiano   _____

5. Herta y Gisela / alemán   _____

6. Luis / mexicano   _____

7. Jean y Guy / francés   _____

8. José Luis / español   _____

EXERCISE E   **Muchas compras** (Many purchases)   Doris went shopping and then met a friend at a cafe. Answer the questions the friend asks about Doris's purchases and the meal.

EXAMPLE: ¿Cómo son los zapatos?   (*cómodo*)   Los zapatos son **cómodos.**

1. ¿Cómo son los aretes?   (*caro*)

   _____

2. ¿Cómo es la falda?   (*corto*)

   _____

3. ¿Cómo es el suéter?   (*grueso*)

   _____

4. ¿Cómo son los chocolates?   (*dulce*)

   _____

5. ¿Cómo son la hamburguesa y las papas fritas?   (*delicioso*)

   _____

6. ¿Cómo son las flores?   (*bonito*)

   _____

7. ¿Cómo es el osito de peluche?   (*suave*)

   _____

b. Position of Adjectives

   (1) Descriptive adjectives generally follow the noun they describe.

un juguete caro	*an expensive toy*
una mujer bondadosa	*a kind woman*
un señor francés	*a French man*

(2) Adjectives expressing quantity or number generally come before the noun they describe.

seis libros	*six books*	**cada vez**	*each time*
muchos dulces	*many candies*	**algunas amigas**	*some friends*

EXERCISE F | **Una sala elegante** (An elegant living room)   Helen is describing the contents of the living room in a friend's new home. Express what she says.

EXAMPLE: sillón / cómodo / dos   Hay **dos sillones cómodos**.

1. sofá / uno / largo   _____

2. chimenea / alto / uno   _____

3. alfombra / uno / elegante   _____

4. lámpara / antiguo / cuatro   _____

5. mesa / redondo / uno   _____

6. flor / mucho / artificial   _____

7. adorno / japonés / alguno   _____

EXERCISE G | **Perdido** (Lost)   Robert misplaced his gym bag and he is reporting it to the security office at the gym. He has to list the items that were in the bag. Express what he says the bag contained.

EXAMPLE: reloj / deportivo / uno   **un reloj deportivo**

1. teléfono / celular / uno   _____

2. toalla / dos / blanco   _____

3. cartera / antiguo / uno   _____

4. llavero / redondo / uno   _____

5. gorra / azul / uno   _____

6. jabón / uno / aromático   _____

2.   Shortening of Adjectives

a. The following adjectives drop the final *-o* when used before a masculine singular noun.

uno	*one, a, an*	*un* **hermano**	*a brother*
bueno	*good*	**un** *buen* **hermano**	*a good brother*

malo *bad*	**un** *mal* **día** *a bad day*
primero *first*	**el** *primer* **hijo** *the first son*
tercero *third*	**el** *tercer* **libro** *the third book*
alguno *some*	*algún* **dinero** *some money*
ninguno *no, not any*	*ningún* **dinero** *no money*

NOTE: 1. The complete form of the adjective is used when

- it follows a masculine singular noun.
  un hermano *bueno* *a good brother*

- it modifies a feminine or plural noun.
  una hermana *buena* *a good sister*
  algunos días *some days*

- a preposition comes between the adjective and the noun.
  el primero de octubre *October 1*

2. The adjectives **alguno** and **ninguno** require an accent mark when the *-o* is dropped: **algún, ningún.**

b. *Ciento* becomes *cien* before any plural noun and before the numbers *mil* (thousand) and *millón* (million). The short form is not used with multiples of *ciento* (*doscientos, trescientos,* etc.) or in combination with any other number (*ciento veinte*).

cien **lápices (plumas)**	*one hundred pencils (pens)*
cien **mil pesetas**	*one hundred thousand pesetas*
cien **millones de personas**	*one hundred million people*

BUT:

trescientos **hombres**	*three hundred men*
seiscientas **comidas**	*six hundred meals*
ciento **ocho pesos**	*one hundred eight pesos*

c. *Grande* becomes *gran* before a singular masculine or feminine noun. When *grande* precedes the noun it means "great."

un *gran* **atleta**	*a great athlete*
una *gran* **actriz**	*a great actress*

d. *Santo* becomes *san* before a man's name, unless the name begins with *Do-* or *To-*.

San **Pedro**	*Saint Peter*
San **Francisco**	*Saint Francis*

BUT:

Santo **Domingo**	*Saint Dominic*
Santo **Tomás**	*Saint Thomas*

NOTE: The feminine form of *santo* is *santa*.

Santa Ana   *Saint Ann*

EXERCISE H   **Premios artísticos** (Artistic awards)   Elena sends this electronic message to a friend about an event that will be televised that evening. Complete each statement with the appropriate form of the word in parentheses.

Esta noche por _____ vez van a presentar _____ premios a
                1. (primero)   2. (uno)

_____ artistas de música, cine y televisión. _____ artista de teatro
    3. (alguno)   4. (Ninguno)

va a recibir _____ premio en esta ceremonia. Dicen que más de _____
              5. (uno)   6. (ciento)

artistas van a volver a casa con _____ premio. La ceremonia va a durar
                                 7. (uno)

_____ ochenta minutos y van a transmitir el programa a más de diez
    8. (ciento)

_____ de casas hispanas. _____ político va a abrir la ceremonia
    9. (millón)   10. (alguno)

desde _____ Francisco pero los artistas van a estar en _____
       11. (Santo)   12. (Santo)

Domingo. Va a ser una _____ noche de gala para todos los artistas hispanos. Por
                   13. (grande)

fin hay _____ _____ programa en la televisión.
     14. (uno)   15. (bueno)

3.   Comparisons

a. To make a comparison of equality, Spanish uses *tan* + adjective (or adverb) + *como* to express *as . . . as.*

Jack es *tan serio como* su hermano.	*Jack is as serious as his brother.*
Nosotros somos *tan cómicos como* tú.	*We are as funny as you.*
Yo corro *tan rápido como* ellos.	*I run as quickly as they.*

b. To make a comparison of equality of nouns, Spanish uses *tanto, (-a)* + noun + *como* to express *as much . . . as* and *tantos, (-as)* + noun + *como* to express *as many . . . as.* *Tanto* agrees in gender and number with the noun that follows it.

Elisa tiene *tanta ropa como* yo.	*Elisa has a much clothing as I.*
Jenny tiene *tantas amigas como* Lisa.	*Jenny has as many friends as Lisa.*

c. To make a comparison of inequality, Spanish uses *más* + adjective (or adverb) + *que* to express *more . . . than*, and *menos* + adjective (or adverb) + *que* to express *less . . . than.*

Jack es *más serio que* su hermano.	*Jack is more serious than his brother.*
Nosotros *somos menos serios* que tú.	*We are less serious than you.*
Yo corro *más (menos) rápido* que ellos.	*I run more (less) quickly than they.*

d. Some adjectives have irregular comparative forms and do not use *más* or *menos* to express a comparison.

ADJECTIVE	COMPARATIVE
bueno *good* **malo** *bad* **pequeño** *small* **grande** *large (great)*	**mejor** *better* **peor** *worse* **menor** *lesser, younger* **mayor** *greater, older*

NOTE: 1. *Mejor* and *peor* generally precede the nouns they modify.

el *mejor* **postre**   *the best dessert*

la *peor* **telenovela**   *the worst soap opera*

2. *Mayor* and *menor* generally follow the nouns they modify.

el hermano *mayor*   *the older brother*

su amiga *menor*   *her youngest friend*

3. The regular and irregular comparative forms of *grande* and *pequeño* have different meanings. *Más grande* and *más pequeño* compare differences in size or height; *mayor* and *menor* compare differences in age or status.

un niño *más pequeño*   *a smaller boy*

un hermano *menor*   *a younger brother*

de *mayor* **(menor) importancia**   *of greater (lesser) importance*

EXERCISE 1   **Personalidades**   Lucy is describing her friends who have many similarities. Express what she says.

EXAMPLE: Sarita / Michelle / bondadoso   Sarita es **tan bondadosa como** Michelle.

1. Adela / Víctor / cómico

_____

2. Glenn / Larry / divertido

_____

3. José y Alfredo / Gerardo / serio

_____

4. Elisa / Myrna / simpático

_____

5. Rafael y Gina / Cathy / independiente

_____

6. Vicky / yo / quieto

_____

7. Rosa / Hugo / diligente

_____

EXERCISE J   **Son iguales.** (They're equal.)   Billy and a friend are talking about how some people do these activities. Express the conclusions they come to.

EXAMPLE: Jack corre rápidamente. Luis corre rápidamente.
Jack corre **tan rápidamente como** Luis.

1. Mi abuelo camina despacio. Mi abuela camina despacio.

   _____

2. Yo grito fuertemente. Michael grita fuertemente.

   _____

3. Álvaro lee cuidadosamente. Nilda lee cuidadosamente.

   _____

4. Vinny y Len silban hábilmente. Fred silba hábilmente.

   _____

5. Jane habla el español bien. Morgan habla el español bien.

   _____

6. Ernesto juega mal al béisbol. Carlos juega mal al béisbol.

   _____

EXERCISE K   **Inventario** (Inventory)   Rather than being specific when asked how many there are of different things, David prefers to compare the quantities he finds on an inventory list. Using the list below, express what David says when asked ¿Cuántos (-as) . . . hay?

EXAMPLE: ¿Cuántos cuchillos hay?   Hay **tantos cuchillos como** cucharas.

1. ¿Cuántos vasos hay?   _____

2. ¿Cuántas servilletas hay?   _____

3. ¿Cuántas tazas hay?   _____

4. ¿Cuántos platos hay?   _____

5. ¿Cuántos saleros hay?   _____

6. ¿Cuántas cucharitas hay?   _____

EXERCISE L	**Ropa nueva** (New clothing) Gladys is shopping with a friend who offers her opinion about what they see in the store. Express what she says.

EXAMPLE: ¿Cuál es más bonito, el suéter negro o el suéter rojo?
           El suéter rojo es **más bonito que** el suéter negro.

1. ¿Cuál es más elegante, la falda larga o la falda corta?

   _____

2. ¿Cuáles son menos calientes, los guantes de piel o los guantes de lana?

   _____

3. ¿Cuáles son más baratos, los zapatos o las sandalias?

   _____

4. ¿Cuál es más larga, la bufanda azul o la bufanda amarilla?

   _____

5. ¿Cuál es menos caro, el vestido gris o el vestido rosado?

   _____

6. ¿Cuál es menos útil, la bolsa grande o la bolsa pequeña?

   _____

7. ¿Cuál es más lujosa, la blusa de lino o la blusa de seda?

   _____

EXERCISE M	**Una encuesta** (A survey) As part of a survey your class is taking, compare the types of television programs listed below using *más* or *menos* and the adjectives provided.

los dibujos animados	aburrido
las noticias	cómico
el pronóstico del tiempo	divertido
las telenovelas	emocionante
los deportes	importante
las películas	interesante

los documentales	popular
las variedades	romántico
las comedias	
los concursos	

EXAMPLE: Los **dibujos animados son más (menos) cómicos que las comedias.**

1. _____

2. _____

3. _____

4. _____

5. _____

6. _____

7. _____

EXERCISE N   ¡**Árbitro!** (Umpire!)   You have been asked to settle a difference of opinion between two friends about how people do things. Using the irregular comparatives *mejor, peor, mayor* and *menor,* give your decision.

EXAMPLE: AMIGO 1:   Lisa canta mal.
AMIGO 2:   Emma canta mal.
TÚ: Emma canta mal.
DECISIÓN: Emma canta peor que Lisa.

1. AMIGO 1:   Jack escribe bien.

   AMIGO 2:   Guy escribe bien.

   TÚ: Jack escribe bien.

   DECISIÓN: _____

2. AMIGO 1:   Luke y Nancy bailan mal.

   AMIGO 2:   Beto y Carmen bailan mal.

   TÚ: Beto y Carmen bailan mal.

   DECISIÓN: _____

3. AMIGO 1:   Nelson tiene veinticinco años.

   AMIGO 2:   Jaime tiene veinte años.

   TÚ: Nelson tiene veinticinco años.

   DECISIÓN: _____

4. AMIGO 1:   Sally patina bien.

   AMIGO 2:   Chris patina bien.

   TÚ: Sally patina bien.

   DECISIÓN: _____

5. AMIGO 1:   Miguel tiene dieciocho años.

   AMIGO 2:   Kim tiene dieciséis años.

   TÚ: Kim tiene dieciséis años.

   DECISIÓN: _____

| EXERCISE O | **Preguntas**   Answer the following questions about yourself and your friends.

1. ¿Tienes tantos amigos como tu mejor amigo?

   _____

2. ¿Quién tiene más hermanos o hermanas, tú o tu mejor amigo?

   _____

3. ¿Eres mayor o menor que tus hermanos?

   _____

4. ¿Cómo son tú y tus hermanos? ¿Simpáticos, cómicos, bondadosos?

   _____

5. ¿Cómo son tú y tus padres? ¿Altos, delgados, fuertes?

   _____

| EXERCISE P | **Semejanzas y diferencias** (Similarities and differences)   Write a paragraph of eight sentences in which you compare and contrast yourself with a friend or sibling using the comparatives of equality and inequality you have learned. You may wish to refer to age, physical characteristics, personality traits and the way in which you do things.

_____

_____

_____

_____

_____

_____

_____

CHAPTER 8
Direct-Object Pronouns

Direct objects tell who or what receives the action of the verb.

Estudio *la lección*.   *I study the lesson.*

Direct-object pronouns replace direct objects and agree with them in gender and number.

Estudio la lección y *la* repaso en casa.   *I study the lesson and review it at home.*

1.   Forms of the Direct-Object Pronouns

SINGULAR	PLURAL
me *me*	**nos** *us*
te *you* (fam.)	**os** *you* (fam.)
lo *him, you* (m., formal); *it* (m.)	**los** *them, you* (m.)
la *her, you* (f., formal); *it* (f.)	**las** *them, you* (f.)
le *him, you*	

NOTE: 1.   In some Spanish-speaking countries, *le* is also used to express *him* and *you.*

2.   The plural form of both *le* and *lo* is *los.*

2.   Position of Direct-Object Pronouns

a. Direct-object pronouns are usually placed directly before the verb.

¿Quién lee el periódico?   *Who reads the newspaper?*
El padre *lo* lee.   *The father reads it.*

¿Tienen Uds. los boletos?   *Do you have the tickets?*
No, nosotros no *los* tenemos.   *No, we don't have them.*

EXERCISE A	**La juguetería** (The toy store) Elvira accompanies some younger cousins to a toy store. As she points out all the things there are, tell what they say using the appropriate direct object pronoun.

EXAMPLE: ¡Jennie, mira la muñeca!   ¡Jennie y Enrique, miren los trenes!

La veo.   **Los** vemos.

1. ¡Jennie, mira los ositos de peluche!

2. ¡Enrique, mira las pelotas de fútbol!

_____

3. ¡Jennie y Enrique, miren los juegos electrónicos!

_____

4. ¡Enrique, mira el monopatín!

_____

5. ¡Jennie, mira los juegos de té!

_____

6. ¡Jennie, mira las casas de muñecas!

_____

7. ¡Enrique y Jennie, miren los juegos de mesa!

_____

8. ¡Jennie, mira el deslizador!

_____

| EXERCISE B | **¿Te falta algo?** (Are you missing something?)   On the way to train station Jeremy's mother asks him again if he packed everything he needs for camp. Express Jeremy's responses using a direct object pronoun in each response.

EXAMPLE: ¿Tienes los anteojos?

Sí, **los** tengo.   OR   No, no **los** tengo.

1. ¿Tienes el cepillo de dientes?   _____

2. ¿Tienes las camisetas?   _____

3. ¿Tienes un suéter?   _____

4. ¿Tienes dinero?   _____

5. ¿Tienes los libros que piensas leer?   _____

6. ¿Tienes los juegos electrónicos?   _____

7. ¿Tienes tu cámara?   _____

8. ¿Tienes tu mochila?   _____

| EXERCISE C | **Con alguna frecuencia** (With some frequency)   Tell with what frequency you do the following things using the appropriate direct object pronoun.

PARA EXPRESARSE MEJOR
La frecuencia

una vez por semana *once a week*
cada (noche, semana, quince días) *every (night, week, two weeks)*
a diario *daily*
de vez en cuando *from time to time*
nunca *never*

EXAMPLE: preparar la tarea   **La** preparo **a diario.**   OR   No la preparo nunca.

1. leer una novela _____

2. comer enchiladas _____

3. ayudar a tus padres _____

4. escuchar discos compactos _____

5. llamar a los amigos por teléfono _____

6. comprar un periódico _____

7. escribir cartas _____

8. gastar dinero _____

EXERCISE D   **¿A quiénes ves?** (Whom do you see?)   You and your sister are talking to your camp counselor at the annual reunion. Answer the counselor's questions using a direct object pronoun.

EXAMPLE: ¿Ves a Carolina y a Mercedes?   Sí, **las** veo.

1. ¿Ves a los hermanos García? _____

2. ¿Ven Uds. a los otros consejeros? _____

3. ¿Y ellos las ven a Uds.? _____

4. ¿Te invitan a otra reunión? _____

5. ¿Ven a Lupe aquí en la reunión? _____

6. ¿Ven los adornos? _____

7. ¿Y Gregorio las visita? _____

b. Direct-object pronouns precede the main verb or are attached to an infinitive.

Lo voy a comprar.
Voy a comprar*lo*. } *I'm going to buy it.*

Él no *las* quiere visitar.
Él no quiere visitar*las*. } *He doesn't want to visit them / you.* (formal)

EXERCISE E   **Preparativos**   Tell who is going to do the following activities in preparation for a family trip. Use a direct object pronoun in your statement.

EXAMPLE: revisar el carro   (*mi papá*)
　　　　　Mi papá **lo va a revisar.**　　OR　　Mi papá **va a revisarlo.**

1. hacer las maletas   (*mi mamá*)

　　_____

2. pagar las cuentas   (*mi papá*)

　　_____

3. renovar el pasaporte   (*yo*)

　　_____

4. sacar fotografías   (*mi hermano*)

　　_____

5. cuidar al perro   (*mi abuela*)

　　_____

6. mandar muchas tarjetas postales   (*mi hermana y yo*)

　　_____

7. perder la bolsa   (*yo*)

　　_____

EXERCISE F   **Preguntas**   Answer the questions a friend asks you using a direct object pronoun in your responses.

EXAMPLE: ¿Vas a ver a Jimmy mañana?
　　　　　Sí, **lo voy a ver** mañana. (Sí, **voy a verlo** mañana.)
　　　　　OR
　　　　　No, **no lo voy a ver** mañana. (No, **no voy a verlo** mañana.)

1. ¿Vas a comer la paella?

　　_____

2. ¿Piensa Ana comprar flores?

　　_____

3. ¿Deben Uds. ayudar a tus padres en casa?

_____

4. ¿Tienes que leer la tarea esta noche?

_____

5. ¿Van tus padres a vender la casa de campo?

_____

6. ¿Tienes que comprar tarjetas de dar gracias?

_____

7. ¿Piensan Uds. visitar un museo durante el viaje?

_____

8. ¿Quieres devolver los libros a la biblioteca?

_____

    c. When used with affirmative commands, direct-object pronouns are attached to the command and an accent mark is usually required on the stressed vowel of the verb in order to keep the original stress. With negative commands, direct-object pronouns come immediately before the command.

    Visíteme.   *Visit me.*

    BUT:

    No *me* visite.   *Don't visit me.*

    NOTE: No accent mark is required if the affirmative command has only one syllable.

        Di. *Say.*   **Dilo.** *Say it.*

EXERCISE G   **Sugerencias** (Suggestions) You and your family are planning a trip. Some cousins who have traveled extensively offer you some suggestions. Express what they say using a direct object pronoun in each case.

EXAMPLE: comprar los boletos   **¡Cómprenlos!**

1. leer las guías turísticas   _____

2. cambiar la moneda   _____

3. visitar los sitios importantes   _____

4. no comprar muchos recuerdos   _____

5. no comer comida exótica   _____

6. saludar a la gente en las tiendas   _____

7. no mandar muchos mensajes electrónicos   _____

8. guardar las cosas bien _____

9. no gastar todo el dinero _____

10. disfrutar el viaje _____

EXERCISE H **Responsabilidades** (Responsibilities) As the day for the outing of the Spanish Club approaches, you remind everyone what they agreed to do. Use a direct object pronoun in each statement.

EXAMPLE: comprar los refrescos   **¡Cómprenlos!**

1. traer el tocadiscos _____

2. escoger los discos compactos _____

3. recoger la comida _____

4. buscar unos juegos _____

5. comprar los platos y los vasos desechables _____

6. preparar los postres _____

7. no olvidar el traje de baño _____

8. no perder el autobús _____

EXERCISE I **Entrevista** (Interview) Answer the questions that a new friend asks. Use a direct object pronoun in each response.

1. ¿Ves la televisión todos los días?

_____

2. ¿Recibes revistas por correo?

_____

3. ¿Cuidas a tus hermanos menores?

_____

4. ¿Compras tu almuerzo en la escuela?

_____

5. ¿Practicas el tenis?

_____

6. ¿Escuchas la música popular en casa?

_____

7. ¿Bebes muchos refrescos?

   _____

8. ¿Invitas a tus amigos a casa?

   _____

9. ¿Celebras tu cumpleaños con una fiesta?

   _____

10. ¿Mandas muchos mensajes electrónicos?

   _____

CHAPTER 9
Indirect-Object Pronouns; *GUSTAR*; Verbs Like *GUSTAR*

1. Indirect-Object Pronouns

Indirect-object pronouns tell to whom or for whom the action of the verb is performed. Indirect-object pronouns replace indirect objects and agree with them in gender and number.

a. Forms of the Indirect-Object Pronouns

SINGULAR	PLURAL
me *to me* **te** *to you* (fam.) **le** *to you* (formal), *to him, to her*	**nos** *to us* **os** *to you* (fam.) **les** *to you* (formal), *to them* (m. and f.)

NOTE: 1. *Le* and *les* are both masculine and feminine indirect-object pronouns.

   2. To clarify meaning or to add emphasis, a phrase with *a* + a prepositional pronoun may be used in addition to the indirect object pronouns.

   (Clarity)   **Yo *les* leo *a ellas.***   *I read to them.*
   (Emphasis)   ***A ti te* llamo más tarde.**   *I'll call you later.*

   Sentences with both indirect object and indirect-object pronoun are very common in Spanish.

   3. *Me, te, nos,* and *os* are also used for direct-object pronouns and for reflexive pronouns.

   4. Indirect-object pronouns may be identified in English by the preposition *to* + a person. The *to* may be expressed or implied.

   ***Les* manda las invitaciones.**   *He sends the invitations to them / you.* (pl.)

b. Position of Indirect-Object Pronouns

   (1) Indirect-object pronouns are usually placed before the verb.

   Juan *nos* habla.   *Juan speaks to us.*
   Ella *le* escribe una carta.   *She writes a letter to him/her/you.* (formal)

EXERCISE A | **Favores** Ricky is very proud of the favors he does for others. Use an indirect-object pronoun to express what he says he does.

EXAMPLE: a la vecina / recoger el correo   **Le recojo el correo.**

1. a mi padre / lavar el carro   _____

2. a ti / prestar la tarea   _____

3. a Uds. / acompañar al centro   _____

4. a nosotros / comprar un refresco   _____

5. a Elena / enseñar un nuevo juego   _____

6. a mis abuelos / ayudar en casa   _____

7. a mi hermano / arreglar el cuarto   _____

EXERCISE B   **Tiempo de regalos** (Gift time)   As the holiday season approaches, Ken tells a friend the gifts he will give his family and friends. Express what he says.

EXAMPLE: comprar una pulsera / a mi mamá   **Le compro** una pulsera a mi mamá

1. dar un libro / a mi papá

   _____

2. mandar una suscripción / a Rebecca y Paul

   _____

3. comprar boletos de teatro / a Vicky y Alicia

   _____

4. regalar una planta / a mi abuela

   _____

5. dar un videojuego / a ti

   _____

6. mandar un disco compacto / a Sergio

   _____

7. regalar una raqueta de tenis / a mi hermana

   _____

EXERCISE C   **La clase**   Terry describes what her teacher does in her class. Express what she says using an indirect-object pronoun.

EXAMPLE: a nosotros / explicar la lección   La maestra **nos** explica la lección.

1. a mí / siempre responder a las preguntas

   _____

2. a Susana / repetir la tarea

   _____

3. a Janet y a Allison / no ayudar con los ejercicios

_____

4. a ti / dar más tiempo en el examen

_____

5. a Luis / enseñar después de la clase

_____

6. a nosotros / prometer muchos premios

_____

7. a los alumnos / decir que son inteligentes

_____

| **EXERCISE D** | **¿A quién(-es)...?** (To whom do you ...?) Manuel wants to know to whom or for whom his friend does various things. Express Manuel's questions and his friend's responses using an indirect-object pronoun.

EXAMPLE: escribir mensajes electrónicos
        ¿A quién le escribes mensajes electrónicos?
        Les escribo mensajes electrónicos a mis primos.

1. hablar en español

_____

_____

2. preparar una comida

_____

_____

3. comprar regalos

_____

_____

4. mandar tarjetas

_____

_____

5. decir la verdad

_____

_____

6. hacer muchas preguntas

_____

_____

7. prestar dinero

_____

_____

(2) When a verb is followed by an infinitive, indirect-object pronouns precede the verb or are attached to the infinitive.

Le **pienso comprar un regalo.**
Pienso comprar*le* **un regalo.** $\Big\}$ *I intend to buy him a gift.*

EXERCISE E   **El Día de las Madres** (Mother's Day) Luz and her sister are describing what they are going to do for their mother and grandmother on Mother's Day. Express what they say using an indirect-object pronoun.

EXAMPLE: a nuestra mamá y abuela / comprar una tarjeta

Les vamos a comprar una tarjeta a nuestra mamá y abuela.
OR:
Vamos a comprar**les** una tarjeta a nuestra mamá y abuela.

1. a nuestra mamá / regalar flores

_____

2. a nuestra abuela / traer chocolates

_____

3. a nuestra mamá y abuela / preparar una comida especial

_____

4. a nuestra abuela / llevar muchos regalos

_____

5. a nuestra mamá y abuela / desear «Felicidades»

_____

6. a nuestra mamá / ofrecer un día de descanso

_____

7. a nuestra mamá y abuela / dar las gracias

_____

EXERCISE F   **¿Cuándo?** A friend asks when you intend to do various things. Express the question and your response, using an indirect-object pronoun. Use the vocabulary presented below in your responses.

PARA EXPRESARSE MEJOR
Expresiones de tiempo

pronto *soon*		**la semana que viene** *next week*	
mañana *tomorrow*		**el año (mes) próximo** *next year (month)*	
pasado mañana *the day after tomorrow*		**esta tarde** *this afternoon, evening*	
esta noche *tonight*		**ahora mismo** *right now*	

EXAMPLE: devolver el videojuego a Tomás

¿Cuándo **le** piensas devolver el videojuego a Tomás?
OR:
¿Cuándo piensas devolver**le** el videojuego a Tomás?

Le pienso devolver el videojuego a Tomás mañana.
OR:
Pienso devolver**le** el videojuego a Tomás mañana.

1. mostrar las fotos a mí

   _____

   _____

2. pagar el dinero a tus padres

   _____

   _____

3. entregar el proyecto a la profesora

   _____

   _____

4. pedir un favor a Carlos y Beto

   _____

   _____

5. prestar el fútbol a tu hermano menor

   _____

   _____

6. cantar «Las mañanitas» a tu primo

   _____

   _____

7. explicar el problema a nosotros

   _____

   _____

8. contar el secreto a tus amigos

_____

_____

| **EXERCISE G** | **Obligaciones**   Martin is quick to remind his friends of their obligations and to tell them what they should do. Express what he says using an indirect-object pronoun. |

EXAMPLE: pedir una disculpa / a sus padres

Les deben pedir una disculpa a sus padres.
OR:
Deben **pedirles** una disculpa a sus padres.

1. devolver las cosas prestadas / a mí

_____

2. explicar las decisiones / a nosotros

_____

3. mostrar los regalos / a los invitados

_____

4. dar una fiesta / a Luisa

_____

5. comprar flores / a la maestra

_____

6. escribir invitaciones / a todos los amigos

_____

7. no decir mentiras / a nadie

_____

(3) The indirect-object pronoun is attached to the end of an affirmative command, but it is placed before a negative command.

Tráiga*me* el dinero.   *Bring me the money.*
BUT:
No me traiga el dinero.   *Don't bring me the money.*

NOTE: When the indirect-object pronoun follows and is attached to the affirmative command, an accent mark is normally required on the stressed vowel of the verb to keep the original stress.

| **EXERCISE H** | **La fiesta**   Express what Mrs. Vidal tells her son's guests they should do at a party in her house. Use an indirect-object pronoun. |

EXAMPLE: Digan «buenas tardes» a nosotros.   **Dígannos** «buenas tardes».

1. No den de comer al perro.

_____

2. Digan «Gracias» a todo el mundo.

_____

3. Ayuden a los compañeros.

_____

4. Muestren cortesía a todos.

_____

5. Expliquen las reglas de los juegos a los niños.

_____

6. Pidan permiso a mi esposo y a mí.

_____

7. Devuelvan los juguetes a mi hijo.

_____

8. No canten a los vecinos.

_____

EXERCISE I   **Uds. no necesitan eso.** (You don't need that.)   Mrs. Sosa has finally gotten her children to help her clean out their playroom. Express what she tells them to do with the things they find.

EXAMPLE: regalar ese juego electrónico / a su primo   **Regálenle** ese juego electrónico.

1. devolver estas fotos / a su abuela   _____

2. dar este osito de peluche / a mí   _____

3. regalar esta muñeca / a su prima   _____

4. dar el camión / a Vicente   _____

5. mostrar esas monedas / a su padre   _____

6. ofrecer la bicicleta / a la vecina   _____

7. mandar estos libros / a sus primos   _____

8. enseñar este juego / a su tío   _____

2.   *GUSTAR*

a. *Gustar* (to please) is used to express "to like."

Me gusta la película.	*I like the film.*
Me gustan los deportes.	*I like sports.*
Nos gusta jugar al béisbol.	*We like to play baseball.*

b. *Gustar* is preceded by an indirect-object pronoun. The form of *gustar* agrees with the subject, which generally follows it.

Le gusta el juguete.	*He (She / You) like(s) the toy.*
Le gustan los juguetes.	*He (She / You) like(s) the toys.*
Nos gusta la canción.	*We like the song.*
Nos gustan las canciones.	*We like the songs.*
Les gusta cantar.	*They like to sing.*

NOTE: If the thing liked is not a noun but an action (expressed by the verb in the infinitive), *gustar* is used in the third-person singular.

| Les *gusta cantar y bailar.* | *They like to sing and dance.* |

c. To clarify the indirect-object pronouns (*le* and *les*) or to give emphasis, the indirect-object normally precedes the indirect object pronoun.

A Carmen no le gusta escribir.	*Carmen doesn't like to write.*
A mis hermanos les gusta comer.	*My brothers like to eat.*
A Rafael le gustan los conciertos.	*Rafael likes the concerts.*
A mí me gusta esquiar.	*I like to ski.*

NOTE: When the indirect-object pronoun is clarified, *a* + noun or *a* + prepositional pronoun is used. The prepositional pronouns are:

PERSONAL PRONOUN	PREPOSITIONAL PRONOUN	PERSONAL PRONOUN	PREPOSITIONAL PRONOUN
yo	*mí*	nosotros	*nosotros*
tú	*ti*	vosotros	*vosotros*
él	*él*	ellos	*ellos*
ella	*ella*	ellas	*ellas*
Ud.	*Ud.*	Uds.	*Uds.*

A la profesora le gusta enseñar.	*The teacher likes to teach.*
A ti te gusta trabajar.	*You like to work.*
A ellos les gustan los libros.	*They like the books.*

3. Verbs Like *GUSTAR*

encantar ⎫
fascinar ⎭ *to delight* (to like a lot or love)

faltar *to be lacking, to need*

parecer *to seem*
doler *to be painful, to cause sorrow*
tocar (a uno) *to be one's turn*

NOTE: Since *parecer* is usually followed by an adjective, the adjective must agree in gender and number with the item described.

La casa me *parece antigua.*	*The house seems old to me.*
Los árboles me *parecen antiguos.*	*The trees seem old to me.*

EXERCISE J   **Gustos**   Some friends are talking about their likes and dislikes. Express what they say.

EXAMPLE: a mí / gustar / los helados   A mí **me gustan** los helados.

1. a Francisco / no gustar / ayudar en casa

   _____

2. a Gwen y a mí / gustar / ir de compras

   _____

3. a ti / no gustar / la comida fría

   _____

4. a Jeff / gustar / la música clásica

   _____

5. a mis hermanos / gustar / practicar los deportes

   _____

6. a Nick y a Felipe / no gustar / gastar dinero

   _____

7. a mí / gustar / pasar el día en el parque

   _____

8. a Uds. / gustar / hablar de otras personas

   _____

9. a nosotros / no gustar / visitar los museos

   _____

10. a Fred / gustar / las comidas exóticas

    _____

EXERCISE K   **Encantos**   Kate is spending the day at the circus with a younger cousin who seems to love everything she sees. Express Kate's questions and her cousin's responses using *encantar* or *fascinar*.

> ## PARA EXPRESARSE MEJOR
> ### El circo   *The circus*
>
> **el globo**   *balloon*   **acróbata** (m. & f.)   *acrobat*
> **entrenador(-ora)**   *trainer*   **payaso(-a)**   *the clown*
> **las palomitas**   *popcorn*   **mago(-a)**   *the magician*

EXAMPLE: gustar / los globos
¿**Te gustan** los globos?
Sí, a mí **me encantan** los globos.

1. gustar / los payasos

_____

_____

2. gustar / las palomitas

_____

_____

3. gustar / el entrenador de leones

_____

_____

4. gustar / la música

_____

_____

5. gustar / los acróbatas

_____

_____

6. gustar / los magos

_____

_____

7. gustar / la visita al circo

_____

_____

EXERCISE L   **Dolores** (Pains)   The school nurse is telling the principal about the students that visited her when they returned from a field trip. Express what she says.

EXAMPLE: a Rocío / doler / las piernas   A Rocío **le duelen** las piernas.

1. a Jaime / doler / el brazo   _____

2. a Kelly y a Emma / doler / los ojos   _____

3. a Lenny / doler / el codo   _____

4. a David y a Oscar / doler / los pies   _____

5. a Ana y a Sally / doler / la garganta   _____

6. a Alfredo / doler / una muela   _____

7. a mí / doler / la cabeza   _____

EXERCISE M   **Una noche de teatro**   Complete the note that Elizabeth writes to a friend about a night she and some friends are planning at the theater. Use the verb indicated and an indirect object pronoun.

Querida Sarita:

El viernes a mis amigas y a mí ——————— ir al teatro. Ya sabes cuánto el teatro
                                    1. (tocar)

——————— a mí. Mi amiga Cristina no puede ir porque a ella ———————
   2. (fascinar)   3. (faltar)

dinero para el boleto. A ella ——————— no poder acompañarnos. A todas mis
                                  4. (doler)

amigas ——————— ir al teatro. A nosotras ——————— una noche de fantasía. A
          5. (encantar)   6. (parecer)

ti ——————— ir al teatro también, ¿verdad? Contéstame pronto.
   7. (gustar)

Tu amiga,

Elizabeth

EXERCISE N   **Un amigo nuevo**   Write eight sentences in Spanish in which you describe your likes and dislikes and those you share with other friends to a new friend. Use the verb *gustar* as well as verbs like *encantar, fascinar,* and *parecer.*

_____

_____

_____

_____

_____

_____

_____

_____

CHAPTER 10

Prepositions; Prepositional Pronouns;
PARA and *POR*

1. Prepositions

Prepositions are words that relate a noun or pronoun to some other word in the sentence.

Lina va *a* la escuela.	*Lina goes to school.*
Yo viajo *con* ellos.	*I travel with them.*
Estudian *en* la clase.	*They study in class.*

a. The Preposition *A*

(1) *A* is used to indicate destination or direction.

Van *a* la ciudad.	*They are going to the city.*
Llegan tarde *a* la fiesta.	*They arrive at the party late.*
El museo está *a* la izquierda.	*The museum is to the left.*

(2) *A* (to) combines with *el* (the) to form the contraction *al* (to the).

Los niños van *al* parque.	*The children go to the park.*
El padre le habla *al* hijo.	*The father speaks to the son.*

> **NOTE:** 1. *A* never combines with the other articles (*la, los, las*) to form a contraction.
>
> | | |
> |---|---|
> | **Yo voy *a la* piscina.** | *I'm going to the pool.* |
> | **El padre les habla *a los* hijos.** | *The father talks to the children.* |
>
> 2. In some expressions, *a* + the definite article are used where there's no equivalent in English.
>
> | | |
> |---|---|
> | **Jugamos *al* tenis.** | *We play tennis.* |

EXERCISE A ¿Adónde van? Tell where each person is going based on the drawing.

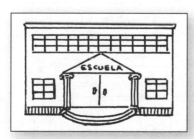

EXAMPLE: Los niños **van a la escuela.**

1. Luke y Felipe _____
   _____ .

2. Sarita y yo _____
   _____ .

3. Yo _____
   _____ .

4. Tú _____
   _____ .

5. Los esquiadores _____
   _____ .

6. Los amigos _____
   _____ .

7. La madre _____
   _____ .

8. La familia _____
   _____ .

9. Janet _____
   _____ .

10. Nora y Luisa _____
    _____ .

(3) *A* is required before the direct object of a verb if the direct object refers to a person, a personalized group, a pet, or something personified. This is known as the "personal *a*."

Ella busca *a* Andrés.	*She looks for Andres.*
Yo veo *al* profesor.	*I see the teacher.*
Nosotros visitamos *a* nuestros amigos.	*We visit our friends.*
Estela cuida *al* gato.	*Estela takes care of the cat.*

BUT:

Ella busca la dirección.	*She looks for the address.*
Yo veo el desfile.	*I see the parade.*

(4) *A* is required before the pronouns *¿quién?*, *¿quiénes?*, *nadie*, and *alguien*, when they refer to a person.

¿*A* quiénes amas?	*Whom do you love?*
No conocen *a* nadie.	*They don't know anyone.*
Veo *a* alguien.	*I see someone.*

NOTE: 1. When used before a direct object, *a* (personal *a*) has no equivalent in English. When used before an indirect object, it is translated as "to."

Visito *a* mi tía.	*I visit my aunt.*
Hablamos *a* la maestra.	*We speak to the teacher.*

2. The personal *a* is not used after the verb *tener* (to have).

Tengo un hermano mayor.	*I have an older brother.*
Tienen muchos primos.	*They have many cousins.*

(5) *A* is used in time expressions to indicate "at."

¿*A* qué hora es la película?	*At what time is the film?*
Es *a* las siete.	*It's at 7 o'clock.*
Te veo *a* las tres.	*I see you at 3 o'clock.*

EXERCISE B   **La reunión escolar**   Tell whom Loretta sees or meets at her school reunion.

EXAMPLE: conocer / el esposo de Anita Vargas   Loretta **conoce al** esposo de Anita Vargas.

1. ver / los artistas del Círculo de Drama

_____

2. conocer / la nueva directora de la escuela

_____

3. ver / todas sus amigas

_____

4. conocer / el novio de María Elena

_____

5. ver / muchos de sus profesores

_____

6. ver / el héroe del equipo de fútbol

_____

EXERCISE C   **El fin de semana**   Tell what these people want to do this weekend.

EXAMPLE: Lola / escuchar / el grupo «Los Reyes» en concierto
Lola quiere escuchar **al** grupo «Los Reyes» en concierto.

1. Tomás / acompañar / su familia

_____

2. Estela / llamar / sus amigas por teléfono

_____

3. mi mamá / visitar / mi tía

_____

4. yo / jugar / tenis

_____

5. Nancy y Sally / ver / una obra de teatro

_____

6. Bill / esperar / sus amigos

_____

7. tú / escuchar / un disco compacto

_____

EXERCISE D   **Preguntas**   Use the cues in parentheses to answer the questions.

1. ¿A qué hora llegas a casa?   (_4:00_)

_____

2. ¿A quiénes saludas en la calle?   (_los vecinos_)

_____

3. ¿Tienes muchos amigos?   (_sí_)

_____

4. ¿A quién buscas en la escuela?   (_mi amiga Elsa_)

_____

5. ¿A quién buscas por la noche? (*nadie*)

_____

6. ¿Admiras tú a una persona famosa? (*sí*)

_____

7. ¿Respetan tus compañeros a los maestros? (*sí*)

_____

8. ¿A quiénes esperas ahora? (*mis padres*)

_____

9. ¿A qué hora comienzan las clases? (*7:30*)

_____

10. ¿Vas a muchas fiestas? (*sí*)

_____

b. The Preposition DE

(1) *De* corresponds to English *of, from,* or *about.*

¿*De* qué hablan?	*What are you talking about?*
Hablamos *de* la película.	*We are speaking about the film.*
Recibe mensajes *de* ellos.	*She receives messages from them.*
Victoria es *de* México.	*Victoria is from Mexico.*
La corbata es *de* seda.	*The tie is made of silk.*

(2) *De* (of, from, about) combines with *el* (the) to form the contraction *del* (of the, from the, about the).

El Sr. Alba es el dueño *del* edificio.	*Mr. Alba is the owner of the building.*
Sacamos dinero *del* banco.	*We take out money from the bank.*

NOTE: *De* never combines with the other articles (*la, los, las*) to form a contraction.

Ellos salen *de* la casa.	*They go out of the house.*

EXERCISE E   **Una charla**   Charlotte overhears the conversations of her classmates in the school cafeteria. Tell what they are speaking about.

EXAMPLE: Gary y Lorenzo / el partido de béisbol
Gary y Lorenzo **hablan del** partido de béisbol.

1. Víctor / la excursión al museo

_____

2. Freddy y Jorge / las elecciones

_____

3. Antonia / los nuevos estilos de ropa

_____

4. Magda y Lina / la tarea

_____

5. Joey / el pronóstico del tiempo

_____

6. yo / las charlas

_____

7. tú y Diana / el nuevo estudiante

_____

EXERCISE F   **Mucho hablar**   Gina tells why she doesn't really enjoy going on school trips. Express what she says.

EXAMPLE: los alumnos / hablar / los otros jóvenes
               Los alumnos **hablan de** los otros jóvenes.

1. la maestra / sacar muchas fotografías / la clase

_____

2. yo / oír / los gritos / los niños

_____

3. la clase / recibir muchas reglas / el director

_____

4. los alumnos / traer mucha comida / la cafetería

_____

5. todo el mundo / abrir las ventanas / el autobús

_____

---

(3) In Spanish, *de* is used to express possession. It is used as follows: noun (thing possessed) + *de* + noun (possessor). This is equivalent to the English possessive expressed with *of*. There is no apostrophe in Spanish to show possession.

el carro del señor Olmeda	*the car of Mr. Olmeda* *Mr. Olmeda's car*
la bicicleta de la niña	*the bicycle of the girl* *the girl's bicycle*
las obras de los autores	*the works of the authors* *the authors' works*

(4) *¿De quién?* and *¿de quiénes?* (Whose?) are used to ask to whom something belongs.

¿De quién son los tenis?	*Whose (sing.) sneakers are they?*
¿De quiénes son los lápices?	*To whom (pl.) do the pencils belong?*

EXERCISE G   **Posesiones**   Tell to whom the following objects belong.

EXAMPLE: el abrigo negro / el profesor   Es el abrigo negro **del** profesor.

1. el calendario / el señor Galindo   _____

2. la computadora / la secretaria   _____

3. la bolsa / la señora Ayala   _____

4. los exámenes / Ricardo   _____

5. el reloj / el consejero   _____

6. la grabadora / la escuela   _____

7. las llaves / Belinda   _____

8. los anteojos / el director   _____

EXERCISE H   **La caja de juguetes** (The toy box)   A young cousin is visiting and sees many toys around the room. As she picks up each toy, she asks to whom they belong. Express her questions and your responses using the cues provided.

EXAMPLE: una muñeca   (*mi hermana menor*)

   ¿De quién es la muñeca? **Es de** mi hermana menor.

1. un rompecabezas   (*Fernando*)

_____

2. un avión   (*el amigo de mi hermano*)

_____

3. un tren   (*el hermano de Silvia*)

_____

4. un monopatín   (*la hija de mi prima*)

_____

5. un libro de cuentos   (*los amigos de Juan*)

_____

6. un osito de peluche   (*el bebé de Gladys*)

_____

(5) A phrase with *de* may also function as an adjective.

la clase *de inglés*	*the English class*
un anillo *de plata*	*a silver ring*

(6) *De + la mañana (la tarde, la noche)* is used following a specific hour to indicate AM or PM.

Son las ocho *de la noche*.	*It's 8:00 PM.*
Salgo a las seis *de la mañana*.	*I leave at 6:00 AM.*

EXERCISE I   **Adivinanzas** (Riddles)   Using the information provided, tell what item is being described.

EXAMPLE: un anillo caro / oro   un anillo caro **de oro**

1. una cadena fina y cara / plata   _____

2. los meses marzo y abril / año   _____

3. una docena / naranjas   _____

4. una corbata fina / seda   _____

5. un suéter caliente / lana   _____

EXERCISE J   **El horario**   Tell at what time you generally do the following activities. Be sure to include the Spanish equivalent of AM or PM in your response.

EXAMPLE: ir a la escuela   Yo voy a la escuela **a las siete de la mañana.**

1. ver tu programa favorito

_____

2. cenar con la familia

_____

3. preparar la tarea

_____

4. decirles «buenos días» a tus padres

_____

5. comer el desayuno

_____

6. hablarles por teléfono a tus amigos

_____

c. The Preposition *EN*

(1) *En* is used to express location. It corresponds to the English *at*, *in*, or *on*.

Ellos están *en* el parque.   *They are at the park.*
Tu bolsa está *en* la silla.   *Your bag is on the chair.*
La silla está *en* el comedor.   *The chair is in the dining room.*

(2) *En* is also used to express means of transportation.

Siempre viajo *en* avión.   *I always travel by plane.*

d. Compound Prepositions

Some prepositions are made up of more than one word.

al lado de *next to*   **después de** *after*
antes de *before*   **detrás de** *behind*
cerca de *near*   **encima de** *on, on top of*
debajo de *under, beneath*   **frente a** *across from, facing*
delante de *in front of*   **lejos de** *far from*
dentro de *within*

EXERCISE K   **Preguntas** A friend calls you on your cellular telephone. Answer the questions she asks you using the cues in parentheses.

1. ¿Dónde estás ahora? (*una fiesta*)

   _____

2. ¿Dónde es la fiesta? (*casa de Diego*)

   _____

3. ¿Cuándo vas a salir de la fiesta? (*diez minutos*)

   _____

4. ¿Cómo viajas? (*tren*)

   _____

5. ¿En cuánto tiempo llegas a casa? (*media hora*)

   _____

6. ¿Sabes dónde vive Martín? (*la Calle Monterrey*)

   _____

EXERCISE L   **En el hotel** Jeremy is very impressed with the hotel he and his family stayed in while they were on vacation. Express what he says with the appropriate compound preposition.

EXAMPLE: el televisor / un armario (*dentro de*)   El televisor está **dentro de** un armario.

1. el cuarto / el ascensor   (*cerca de*)

   _____

2. la lámpara / un escritorio   (*encima de*)

   _____

3. la piscina / el café   (*frente a*)

   _____

4. el refrigerador / una mesa   (*debajo de*)

   _____

5. el gimnasio / el cuarto   (*lejos de*)

   _____

6. el teléfono / la cama   (*al lado de*)

   _____

7. la cancha de tenis / el hotel   (*detrás de*)

   _____

2.   Prepositional Pronouns

When a personal pronoun follows a preposition, it takes the following forms:

SINGULAR	PLURAL
mí *me* **ti** *you* (familiar) **usted (Ud.)** *you* **él** *him, it* **ella** *her, it*	**nosotros, -as** *us* **vosotros, -as** *you* (familiar) **ustedes (Uds.)** *you* **ellos** *them* (m.) **ellas** *them* (f.)

a. Prepositional pronouns are used as the objects of a preposition and always follow the preposition.

| **No es de *él*; es de *ella*.** | *It's not his; it's hers.* |
| **Es para *mí*; no es para *ellos*.** | *It's for me; it's not for them.* |

b. *Mí* and *ti* combine with the preposition *con* as follows:

conmigo *with me*   **contigo** *with you*

NOTE: 1.   Prepositional pronouns are identical to subject pronouns, except for *mí* and *ti*.

2.   The forms *conmigo* and *contigo* do not change in gender and number.

3.   The familiar plural form *vosotros, -as* is used in Spain but rarely in Spanish America, where the form *ustedes* (*Uds.*) is preferred.

c. Common Prepositions

a *to, at*	**entre** *between, among*
cerca de *near*	**hacia** *toward*
con *with*	**para** *for*
contra *against*	**por** *for*
de *of, from*	**sin** *without*
en *in, on*	**sobre** *on top of, over*

EXERCISE M   **Cambio de planes** (A change of plans)   Elena writes her friend this e-mail message about a change in plans. Complete the message with the appropriate prepositional pronouns.

Querida Linda:

Yo no puedo ir al cine con _____ 1. . Yo tengo que ir de compras y mi mamá va a ir

con _____ 2. . Es el cumpleaños de papá, y mamá quiere comprar algo para

_____ 3. . A _____ 4. le gustan mucho los libros de arte y

a _____ 5. me gustan también. No podemos regresar a casa sin _____ 6.

porque es lo único que planeamos comprarle.

¿Conoces el Almacén Vasconia? Hay una librería famosa cerca de _____ 7. .

Quizás podemos encontrar el libro en esa librería. Lamento este cambio de planes pero si a

_____ 8. te parece una buena idea, tú puedes ir con _____ 9. .

Espero tu respuesta.

Hasta pronto,

Elena

EXERCISE N   **Preguntas**   Answer your friend's questions using a prepositional pronoun in your responses.

EXAMPLE: ¿Hablas con Luis y Paco? (*sí*)   **Sí,** hablo **con ellos.**

1. ¿Vas a cenar en casa de Carmen y Manuel? (*sí*)

_____

2. ¿Van tus padres contigo? (*sí*)

_____

3. ¿Pueden ir tus padres sin ti? (*no*)

_____

4. ¿Viven Carmen y Manuel cerca del campo de golf?   (*sí*)

   _____

5. ¿Hay una estatua grande en el jardín?   (*no*)

   _____

6. ¿Piensas comprar flores para Carmen?   (*sí*)

   _____

7. ¿Va tu hermano por Uds. más tarde?   (*no*)

   _____

3.   *PARA* and *POR*

Both *para* and *por* have similar meanings in English. In Spanish, however, the use of *para* or *por* depends on the context. Their meanings in English may vary with the context.

a. *Para* is used to:

(1) express a purpose or goal.

Estudia *para* dentista.	*She studies to be a dentist.*
Ahorro *para* comprar un carro.	*I am saving in order to buy a car.*
Comemos *para* vivir.	*We eat to live.*

(2) express destination or direction.

Salen *para* Madrid.	*They are leaving for Madrid.*
La flecha apunta *para* la izquierda.	*The arrow points to the left.*

(3) indicate a time or date in the future.

Esta tarea es *para* mañana.	*This assignment is for tomorrow.*
Van a llegar *para* las seis.	*They are going to arrive by six o'clock.*

(4) express *for* or *considering that*, when comparing a person, object, or situation with others of its kind.

***Para* niño, grita mucho.**	*For a child, he shouts a lot.*
***Para* americano, habla bien el español.**	*For an American, he speaks Spanish well.*

b. *Por* is used to:

(1) express *in exchange for*.

Pago cinco dólares *por* el libro.	*I pay five dollars for the book.*
Cambio esta blusa *por* ese suéter.	*I exchange this blouse for that sweater.*

(2) express *along, through, by*, and *around*, after a verb of motion.

Entran *por* la otra puerta.	*They enter through the other door.*
Anda *por* el lago.	*He walks around the lake.*
Siempre paso *por* la escuela.	*I always pass by the school.*

(3) express the duration of an action.

Practica el piano *por* tres horas.   *She practices the piano for three hours.*

Common Expressions with POR

por ejemplo *for example*   **por la tarde** *in the afternoon*
por eso *that's why*   **por lo general** *generally*
por favor *please*   **por lo menos** *at least*
por fin *finally, at last*   **por supuesto** *of course*
por la mañana *in the morning*   **por todas partes** *everywhere*
por la noche *at night, in the night* **por el río** *along the river*

| EXERCISE O | **Muchos regalos** Nick is showing Silvia the gifts he bought in Mexico and is telling her for whom each one is. Silvia repeats what he says with a slight change. Express what she says using *para* and an appropriate prepositional pronoun. |

EXAMPLE: La cartera es para Elena.   La cartera es para **ella.**

1. El llavero es para Benito.   _____

2. La figura es para Jane y Bill.   _____

3. Los huaraches son para Keith.   _____

4. El sombrero es para Nick.   _____

5. Los aretes son para Silvia.   _____

6. Las pulseras son para Clara y Rosita. _____

7. Los calendarios son para Silvia y Nick. _____

| EXERCISE P | **Una visita al museo** Complete the following message that Tom received from a friend who has just returned from a visit to the museum. |

Cuando llegan al museo, deben entrar _____ la puerta principal y caminar
                                          1.

_____ el gran salón de entrada hasta la caja. Allí deben pagar cinco
    2.

dólares _____ persona _____ la entrada a la exposición especial.
            3.   4.

Hay un guía que va a acompañarlos _____ la exposición especial _____
                                      5.   6.

una hora. Después pueden caminar solos _____ todos los salones del museo. En
                                            7.

la tienda de recuerdos del museo pueden cambiar su boleto de entrada _____ un
                                                                          8.

cartel de la exposición especial.

EXERCISE Q   **¿Para o por?**   Complete this conversation between Adela and Teresa with either *por* or *para*.

ADELA: ¿Qué planes tienes _____ hoy _____ la tarde? Son interesantes y divertidos, _____ supuesto.

TERESA: Emma y yo vamos al centro _____ la tarde _____ almorzar juntas. _____ supuesto, tú puedes ir también.

ADELA: Muchas gracias _____ la invitación pero Uds. van a charlar _____ dos horas _____ lo menos.

TERESA: _____ lo general, yo no almuerzo _____ la tarde.

ADELA: ¿Quién va _____ ella?

TERESA: Su mamá.

ADELA: ¿Tienen otros planes _____ otro día?

TERESA: Sí, _____ el sábado próximo tenemos boletos _____ ver una obra de teatro. _____ fin vamos a ver esa obra tan popular. _____ ver la obra bien, pagamos treinta dólares _____ los boletos.

ADELA: El domingo _____ la mañana te voy a llamar _____ teléfono _____ saber de la obra.

TERESA: Llámame _____ la tarde, _____ favor. Los domingos me gusta dormir _____ la mañana.

EXERCISE R   **Mi barrio** (My neighborhood)   Write ten sentences in which you tell where different stores, important buildings, and sports facilities in your neighborhood are located in relation to each other.

_____

_____

_____

_____

_____

_____

_____

_____

_____

CHAPTER 11
Verbs Irregular in the Present Tense

1. Verbs with Irregular *YO* Forms

a. The following verbs are irregular only in the first-person singular (*yo*) form in the present tense:

hacer *to make, do*	poner *to put, place*	saber *to know*	salir *to go out*	ver *to see; to watch*
hago	pongo	sé	salgo	veo
haces	pones	sabes	sales	ves
hace	pone	sabe	sale	ve
hacemos	ponemos	sabemos	salimos	vemos
hacéis	ponéis	sabéis	salís	veis
hacen	ponen	saben	salen	ven

b. The verbs *caer* (to fall) and *traer* (to bring) have an *i* between the stem and the *yo* ending (-*go*). Their other present tense forms are regular.

caer	*to fall*	traer	*to bring*
caigo	caemos	traigo	traemos
caes	caéis	traes	traéis
cae	caen	trae	traen

EXERCISE A | **Los aparatos eléctricos** Gladys is telling how she and her family enjoy using their new appliances. Tell how they use them.

PARA EXPRESARSE MEJOR
Los aparatos eléctronicos

el lavaplatos *dishwasher*

la lavadora *washing machine*

la secadora *clothes drier*

el horno de microondas *microwave oven*

la licuadora *blender*

el horno *oven*

el congelador *freezer*

la tostadora *toaster*

EXAMPLE: Gladys / la fruta / la licuadora   Gladys **pone** la fruta **en** la licuadora.

1. yo / la ropa sucia / la lavadora

2. mi mamá / los vasos / el lavaplatos

_____

3. mi hermano / el pan / la tostadora

_____

4. Nelson y yo / el helado / el congelador

_____

5. tú / la comida / el horno de microondas

_____

6. mi abuela / el pavo / el horno

_____

7. Gladys y Marta / la ropa mojada / la secadora

_____

EXERCISE B   **Una cena mexicana**   Roberto and his friends are planning a Mexican dinner. Tell what each person makes for the dinner.

EXAMPLE: Roberto / tacos   Roberto **hace** tacos.

1. tú / una ensalada de frutas   _____

2. Ruth / un pastel   _____

3. yo / quesadillas   _____

4. Roberto y yo / enchiladas   _____

5. Greta y Lance / pollo con mole   _____

6. Enrique / frijoles   _____

EXERCISE C   **Nosotros sabemos mucho.**   Hilda is babysitting her young cousins. They are eager to tell her who knows what. Express what they say.

EXAMPLE: Freddy / el alfabeto   Freddy **sabe** el alfabeto.

1. yo / contar de uno a diez

_____

2. Luis / muchos cuentos

_____

3. Carla y yo / patinar en hielo

_____

4. tú / un chiste

_____

5. Vicente y Pablo / usar la computadora

_____

6. Eileen / los meses del año

_____

EXERCISE D   **¡Todos a la playa!**   Felice and some friends are going to the beach. Tell what each one brings.

EXAMPLE: Felice / aceite de broncear   Felice **trae** aceite de broncear.

1. Javier / una pelota de voleibol

_____

2. yo / la radio

_____

3. Leonardo y Jack / el tocador de discos compactos

_____

4. tú / las toallas

_____

5. Evelyn / una sábana

_____

6. Felice y yo / los refrescos

_____

EXERCISE E   **Soy organizada.**   Alicia has learned the importance of being neat. Complete the paragraph she writes with the appropriate form of the verbs indicated.

Yo _____ que es importante ser organizada. Yo _____ mis juguetes a
          1. (saber)   2. (traer)

mi cuarto y los _____ en los estantes. Si un juguete _____ al suelo,
                      3. (poner)   4. (caer)

lo _____ en el estante otra vez. Si yo no _____ estas cosas no
        5. (poner)   6. (hacer)

_____ con mis amigas y no _____ mis programas favoritos.
      7. (salir)   8. (ver)

2. Verbs with Irregular Present-Tense Forms

The verbs *oír, decir, tener,* and *venir* are irregular in the present tense.

oír to hear; to listen	decir to say, tell	tener to have	venir to come
oigo	digo	tengo	vengo
oyes	dices	tienes	vienes
oye	dice	tiene	viene
oímos	decimos	tenemos	venimos
oís	decís	tenéis	venís
oyen	dicen	tienen	vienen

EXERCISE F   **Vamos a casa.**   Everyone is coming home for the holidays, but on a different day. Tell when each person is coming home.

EXAMPLE: Marcos / el lunes   Marcos **viene** el lunes.

1. Omar y Catarina / el sábado   _____

2. tú / el miércoles   _____

3. Ronald y yo / el viernes   _____

4. Doris / el jueves   _____

5. Federica / el martes   _____

6. yo / el domingo   _____

EXERCISE G   **¿Qué oyen?**   A group of friends are walking around the city and each one hears something different. Tell what each person hears.

EXAMPLE: Alex / un avión   Alex **oye** un avión.

1. Mike y Tom / un grito   _____

2. yo / muchas voces   _____

3. Mario y yo / música   _____

4. tú / el motor de un autobús   _____

5. Beto / risas extrañas   _____

6. Tina / el cantar de los pájaros   _____

EXERCISE H   **Mandados** (Errands)   Using the expression *tener que,* tell what errands each of the following people has to do.

EXAMPLE: Ricardo / comprar un regalo   Ricardo **tiene que** comprar un regalo.

1. Vanessa y yo / ir al supermercado

   _____

2. tú / ir al correo

   _____

3. Luz y Dora / devolver un video

   _____

4. yo / ir a la florería

   _____

5. Jeremy / comprar boletos para un concierto

   _____

6. Michelle y Emma / sacar dinero del banco

   _____

EXERCISE I   **¿Quién dice? ¿Quién tiene razón?**   Rafael and Pilar had a quarrel and their friends have something to say about it. Write what they say.

EXAMPLE: Elvira / decir / Pilar / tener razón   Elvira **dice que** Pilar **tiene** razón.

1. Norma y yo / decir / Rafael / no tener razón

   _____

2. Lorenzo / decir / Pilar / tener razón

   _____

3. yo / decir / los dos / tener razón

   _____

4. June / decir / yo / tener razón

   _____

5. tú / decir / Rafael y Pilar / no tener razón

   _____

6. nosotros / decir / Uds. / tener razón

   _____

7. Pilar / decir / nosotros / tener razón

   _____

3. Expressions with *TENER*

¿Qué *tienes*?	*What's the matter with you?*
¿Qué *tiene* Pablo?	*What's the matter with Pablo?*

tener... años — *to be . . . years old*
¿Cuántos años *tienen* Uds.? — *How old are you?*
Nosotros *tenemos* quince años. — *We are fifteen years old.*

tener (mucho) calor — *to be (very) warm [persons]*
Mi abuela *tiene* calor. — *My grandmother is warm.*

tener cuidado — *to be careful*
¡*Ten* cuidado en el parque! — *Be careful in the park!*

tener dolor de cabeza — *to have a headache*
Yo *tengo* dolor de cabeza. — *I have a headache.*

tener dolor de muelas — *to have a toothache*
Ella *tiene* dolor de muelas. — *She has a toothache.*

tener (mucho) frío — *to be (very) cold [persons]*
Mi hermano *tiene* frío. — *My brother is cold.*

tener ganas de — *to feel like, want to*
El niño *tiene* ganas de correr. — *The boy feels like running.*

tener (mucha) hambre — *to be (very) hungry*
Ellos no *tienen* hambre ahora. — *They are not hungry now.*

tener miedo de — *to be afraid of*
El niño *tiene* miedo del juguete. — *The boy is afraid of the toy.*

tener (mucha) sed — *to be (very) thirsty*
Yo *tengo* mucha sed. — *I am very thirsty.*

tener (mucho) sueño — *to be (very) sleepy*
Tenemos sueño. — *We are sleepy.*

tener prisa — *to be in a hurry*
¿Por qué *tienes* prisa? — *Why are you in a hurry?*

tener que + infinitive — *to have to, must*
El alumno *tiene que* estudiar. — *The student has to study.*

tener razón / no *tener* razón — *to be right / to be wrong*
Tú siempre *tienes* razón. — *You are always right.*
Yo no *tengo* razón. — *I'm wrong.*

EXERCISE J **Causa y efecto** Tell what causes these people to do what they do. Use an expression with *tener*.

EXAMPLE: José contesta la pregunta y gana un premio.   José **tiene razón**.

1. Yo duermo la siesta.

_____

2. Mi padre corre para llegar a tiempo.

_____

3. Kira visita al dentista.

_____

4. Los niños piden un sándwich.

_____

5. La maestra toma dos aspirinas.

_____

6. Valerie y yo vamos a la playa.

_____

7. Mi abuela usa guantes.

_____

8. Yo voy a un baile.

_____

9. Tú nadas en la piscina.

_____

10. Las señoras gritan al ver el ratoncito.

_____

11. Manolo aprende a manejar.

_____

12. Hay un examen en la clase de ciencia de Elena.

_____

4.   *DAR* **and** *IR*

	dar *to give*	ir *to go*
yo	doy	voy
tú	das	vas
Ud., él, ella	da	va
nosotros, -as	damos	vamos
vosotros, -as	dais	vais
Uds., ellos, ellas	dan	van

NOTE: A conjugated form of *ir* + *a* + an infinitive is used to express a future action.

Ella *va a trabajar.*   *She is going to work.*

¿Cuándo *vamos a nadar?*   *When are we going to swim?*

EXERCISE K   **¿Qué dan?**   Answer the questions using the cues in parentheses.

EXAMPLE: ¿Qué le da la madre al niño?   (*un osito de peluche*)

La madre le **da** un osito de peluche al niño.

1. ¿Qué le das tú a tu abuela?   (*dulces*)

   _____

2. ¿Qué le dan Uds. a la maestra?   (*la tarea*)

   _____

3. ¿Qué les da Greg a sus padres?   (*las gracias*)

   _____

4. ¿Qué les dan Analuz y Rocío a los perros?   (*un hueso*)

   _____

5. ¿Qué le dan Héctor y José a la mesera?   (*una propina*)

   _____

6. ¿Qué les da el profesor a los alumnos?   (*muchos exámenes*)

   _____

7. ¿Qué le doy yo al cajero en la tienda?   (*mi tarjeta de crédito*)

   _____

EXERCISE L   **Un día ocupado**   Everyone in the Rivera family has a different destination today. Tell where each person is going.

EXAMPLE: el señor Rivera / la oficina   El señor Rivera *va* a la oficina.

1. Esteban y Larry / el gimnasio   _____

2. Rebecca / una fiesta de cumpleaños   _____

3. yo / el jardín botánico   _____

4. la abuela / el salón de belleza   _____

5. tú / el aeropuerto   _____

6. Miguel y yo / el centro comercial   _____

7. Pedro y Pablo / las montañas   _____

EXERCISE M   ¿Adónde vas, qué vas a hacer y por qué?   Write a paragraph of eight sentences in which you tell where you are going this weekend, why you are going there, and what you are going to do. Use as many of the irregular verbs from this chapter as you can.

_____

_____

_____

_____

_____

_____

_____

CHAPTER 12
Expressing the Future Using *IR* + *A* + Infinitive; Time Expressions

1. *IR* + *A* + **Infinitive**

An action in the future can be expressed in Spanish by the present tense of *ir* followed by the preposition *a* and the infinitive of the verb that indicates the future action.

¿Qué *van a hacer* mañana?   *What are you going to do tomorrow?*

***Vamos a jugar* al fútbol mañana.**   *We're going to play football tomorrow.*

EXERCISE A   **Las vacaciones**   Jean and Nancy are talking about what their friends are going to do during the vacation. Express what they say.

EXAMPLE: Amir / trabajar en un restaurante   Amir **va a trabajar** en un restaurante.

1. Jennifer / aprender a conducir

   _____

2. Les y Vince / jugar en el equipo de béisbol

   _____

3. Alicia / cuidar a su hermanita

   _____

4. yo / hacer un viaje a Colombia

   _____

5. tú / tomar una clase de baile moderno

   _____

6. Blanca y yo / ir de compras

   _____

7. Selene / descansar en casa

   _____

EXERCISE B   **En el futuro**   Tell when these people will do the activities indicated. Use the expressions provided below and the *ir a* + infinitive construction.

> ## PARA EXPRESARSE MEJOR
> ### Tiempo futuro *Future time*
>
> | | |
> |---|---|
> | **más tarde** *later* | **después** *later* |
> | **por la mañana** *in the morning* | **esta mañana** *this morning* |
> | **por la tarde** *in the afternoon* | **esta tarde** *this afternoon* |
> | **por la noche** *at night* | **esta noche** *tonight* |
> | **mañana** *tomorrow* | **pasadomañana** *the day after tomorrow* |
> | **la semana (el mes, el año) que viene** *next week (month, year)* | |

EXAMPLE: Celia / viajar en barco   Celia **va a viajar** en barco el año que viene.

1. yo / jugar al tenis

_____

2. Jacques / comprar una computadora

_____

3. Elizabeth y yo / aprender a esquiar

_____

4. tú / ver tu programa favorito

_____

5. los muchachos / escuchar música

_____

6. Anita y Carlos / preparar la tarea

_____

7. nosotros / hablar con un amigo por teléfono

_____

8. Sergio / montar en bicicleta

_____

EXERCISE C	**Las circunstancias** Circumstances affect what people will do. Use *ir a* + infinitive to tell what you will or will not do in the following circumstances.

leer una novela	ir a la playa	llamarlo por teléfono
ir con ellos	dormir hasta tarde	salir de la casa
ahorrar el dinero	asistir a la escuela	ver al médico

EXAMPLE: Si llueve, **voy a** leer una novela.

1. Si hace mucho calor, _____ .

2. Si no tengo dinero, _____ .

3. Si mi amigo no me llama, _____ .

4. Si mis padres van al campo, _____ .

5. Si mañana es día de fiesta, _____ .

6. Si quiero comprar algo especial, _____ .

7. Si nieva mucho, _____ .

8. Si estoy enfermo, _____ .

EXERCISE D   **Un fin de semana largo**   Write eight sentences in which you describe what you are going to do during a long weekend.

_____

_____

_____

_____

_____

_____

_____

_____

2.   Time Expressions

a.   *¿Qué hora es?* is equivalent to "What time is it?"

b.   In expressing time, "It's" is expressed by *Es la* (for one o'clock) and *Son las* for other hours (five o'clock, six o'clock, and so on.).

Es la una.	*It's one o'clock.*
Son las cinco (seis).	*It's five (six) o'clock.*

c.   Time after (or past) the hour, up to half past, is expressed by the hour + *y*, followed by the number of minutes. "Half past" is expressed by *y media;* "a quarter past" is expressed by *y cuarto.*

Es la una y veinte.	*It's twenty (minutes) after one. It's 1:20.*
Son las tres y media.	*It's half past three. It's 3:30.*
Son las ocho y cuarto.	*It's a quarter after eight. It's 8:15.*

d. After half past, the time is expressed in terms of the following hour + *menos* (minus) + the minutes.

Son las *cinco menos diez*.   *It's ten minutes to five. It's 4:50.*
Son las *once menos cuarto*.   *It's a quarter to eleven. It's 10:45.*

e. The expression *de la mañana* corresponds to English AM (in the morning). *De la tarde* (in the afternoon) and *de la noche* (in the evening) correspond to English PM. *En punto* means *sharp* or *on the dot*.

Son las siete *de la mañana*.   *It's 7:00 AM.*
Es la una *de la tarde*.   *It's 1:00 PM.*
Son las diez *de la noche en punto*.   *It's 10:00 PM sharp.*

> **NOTE:** 1. Instead of *media* and *cuarto*, the number of minutes may be used (*treinta, quince*).
>
> **Son las cuatro *y treinta*.**   *It's four-thirty. It's half past four.*
> **Es la una *y quince*.**   *It's one-fifteen. It's a quarter past one.*
>
> 2. It's not uncommon to hear times like 2:40 and 2:45 expressed with *y*.
> **Son las dos *y cuarenta*.**   *It's two-forty.*
> **Son las dos *y cuarenta y cinco*.** *It's two-forty-five.*

f. Common Time Expressions

¿Qué hora es?	*What time is it?*	**a mediodía**	*at noon*
¿A qué hora?	*At what time?*	**Es medianoche.**	*It's midnight.*
a las ocho (nueve)	*at eight (nine) o'clock*	**a medianoche**	*at midnight*
de la mañana	*in the morning,* AM	**Es tarde.**	*It's late.*
de la tarde	*in the afternoon,* PM	**a tiempo**	*on time*
de la noche	*in the evening,* PM	**en punto**	*exactly, sharp*
Es mediodía.	*It's noon.*		

EXERCISE E	**¿Qué hora es?** You are in a clock store and notice that every clock has a different time. Express the hours indicated on the clocks.

EXAMPLE: **Son las once y media.**

ESCUELA

1. _____   2. _____

3. _____

7. _____

4. _____

8. _____

5. _____

9. _____

6. _____

10. _____

EXERCISE F   **¿A qué hora?**   Tell at what time in the morning, afternoon, or evening you usually do the following activities.

EXAMPLE: desayunar   Yo **desayuno a las siete de la mañana.**

1. practicar un deporte

   _____

2. hablar por teléfono con un amigo

   _____

3. saludar a tus padres

   _____

4. preparar la tarea

   _____

5. ver tu programa favorito

_____

6. comer con los amigos

_____

7. ir a la clase de inglés

_____

8. salir de la escuela

_____

9. ayudar a tu madre

_____

10. decirles «buenas noches» a tus padres

_____

EXERCISE G   **¿A qué hora van a llegar?**   Members of your family are coming to a reunion at your house. Tell at what time each one is going to arrive based on the information given.

EXAMPLE: Mis abuelos viajan en avión. El vuelo sale a las diez y diez de la mañana y dura dos horas y veinticinco minutos. ¿A qué hora van a llegar?
Van a llegar a la una menos veinticinco.

1. Tu hermano viaja en autobús. El autobús sale a las tres y cuarto de la tarde y el viaje dura seis horas y quince minutos. ¿A qué hora va a llegar?

_____

2. Tu tía viaja en carro. Sale de su casa a las once menos diez de la mañana y el viaje dura una hora y diez minutos. ¿A qué hora va a llegar?

_____

3. Tus primos Felipe y Jorge viajan en tren. El tren sale a las dos y veinte de la tarde y el viaje dura cinco horas y cuarenta minutos. ¿A qué hora van a llegar?

_____

4. Tu prima viene en carro. Sale de su casa a las siete y diez de la noche y el viaje dura cuarenta minutos. ¿A qué hora va a llegar?

_____

5. Tus tíos vienen en avión. El vuelo sale a las nueve menos veinte de la noche y el vuelo dura una hora y cincuenta y cinco minutos. ¿A qué hora van a llegar?

_____

| EXERCISE H | **Cosas que vamos a hacer**   You and your siblings have promised your parents that you are going to do all the chores they have been asking you to do. Write eight sentences in Spanish in which you tell the chores you are going. Include at what time you are going to do them. |

_____

_____

_____

_____

_____

_____

_____

_____

CHAPTER 13
Demonstrative Adjectives; Demonstrative Pronouns

1. Demonstrative Adjectives

Demonstrative adjectives, like other adjectives, agree with their nouns in gender (masculine or feminine) and number (singular or plural).

	MASCULINE	FEMININE	MEANING
SINGULAR	*este* niño	*esta* niña	*this*
PLURAL	*estos* niños	*estas* niñas	*these*

	MASCULINE	FEMININE	MEANING
SINGULAR	*ese* niño	*esa* niña	*that*
PLURAL	*esos* niños	*esas* niñas	*those*

	MASCULINE	FEMININE	MEANING
SINGULAR	*aquel* niño	*aquella* niña	*that* (at a distance)
PLURAL	*aquellos* niños	*aquellas* niñas	*those* (at a distance)

NOTE:

1. *Este* (*esta, estos, estas*) refers to what is near. *Ese* (*esa, esos, esas*) refers to what isn't so near. *Aquel* (*aquella, aquellos, aquellas*) refers to what is remote from both the speaker and the person addressed.

Esta camisa es bonita.	*This shirt is pretty.*
Me gusta *esa* camisa que tienes en la mano.	*I like that shirt that you have in your hand.*
No me gusta *aquella* camisa.	*I don't like that shirt over there.*

2. The adverbs *aquí* (here), *ahí* (there), and *allí* ([over] there) correspond to the demonstrative adjectives *este, ese,* and *aquel,* respectively.

esta lámpara (aquí)   *this lamp (here)*

Pon $\begin{cases} \text{esa lámpara ahí.} \\ \text{aquella lámpara allí.} \end{cases}$ Put $\begin{cases} \text{that lamp there.} \\ \text{that lamp over there.} \end{cases}$

EXERCISE A   **El catálogo**   Adriana is looking through a museum gift shop catalog. Express what she says about some of the items she sees in the catalog.

EXAMPLE: plato   Me gusta **este** plato.

1. tarjetas _____

2. carteles _____

3. estatua _____

4. pisapapeles _____

5. vasos _____

6. anillo _____

7. bufandas _____

8. caja de música _____

EXERCISE B ¿Qué te parece ...? Gina wants Ruth's opinion on various things they see in a store. Express Gina's question and Ruth's responses.

EXAMPLE: blusas / feas
¿Qué te parecen estas blusas?
Esas blusas son feas.

1. botas / cómodas

_____

_____

2. abrigo / caro

_____

_____

3. falda / muy larga

_____

_____

4. bolsa / bonita

_____

_____

5. cinturón / barato

_____

_____

6. vestido / elegante

_____

_____

7. guantes / finos

_____

_____

8. sombrero / cómico

_____

_____

EXERCISE C   **De paseo** Jimmy and his family are driving through the countryside and pass through a small town. Express Jimmy's comments about the things he sees through the car window.

EXAMPLE: tienda / interesante   **Aquella** tienda es interesante.

1. iglesia / muy antigua   _____

2. casa / grande   _____

3. lago / tranquilo   _____

4. monumento / formidable   _____

5. calles / estrechas   _____

6. restaurante / popular   _____

7. árboles / altos   _____

8. perro / bonito   _____

EXERCISE D   **De compras** Lucy is shopping for gifts and tells the store clerk what she wants to look at. Express what she says.

PARA EXPRESARSE MEJOR
Telas y diseños _Fabrics and designs_

la seda _silk_	**la lana** _wool_
el lino _linen_	**la plata** _silver_
el cuero / la piel _leather_	**a rayas** _striped_
el algodón _cotton_	**a cuadros** _plaid_

EXAMPLE: el suéter rojo / ahí   **Quiero ver ese** suéter rojo.

1. la corbata de seda / aquí   _____

2. los pañuelos de lino / allí   _____

3. la camisa de rayas / ahí   _____

4. la cartera negra / allí   _____

5. el cinturón de piel / aquí   _____

6. el llavero de plata / allí   _____

7. los pantalones de algodón / ahí _____

8. las botas negras / aquí _____

9. el chaleco de lana / aquí _____

10. la bufanda a cuadros / allí _____

| EXERCISE E | **Muchas preguntas** Terri accompanies her grandmother when she goes food shopping. Her grandmother is always asking the price of everything she sees. Express her grandmother's questions and the clerk's responses. |

EXAMPLE: pan / ahí / $1.00
            ¿Cuánto cuesta ese pan?
            Este pan cuesta un dólar.

1. manzanas / allí / $3.00

    _____

    _____

2. piña / aquí / $5.00

    _____

    _____

3. zanahorias / ahí / $2.00

    _____

    _____

4. pastel / aquí / $7.00

    _____

    _____

5. helado / ahí / $6.00

    _____

    _____

6. plátanos / allí / $2.00

    _____

    _____

7. chuletas de cerdo / aquí / $8.00

    _____

    _____

8. galletas / ahí / $5.00

    _____

    _____

2.   Demonstrative Pronouns

Demonstrative pronouns, like other pronouns, agree with the nouns they replace in gender (masculine or feminine) and number (singular or plural).

Demonstrative pronouns are distinguished from demonstrative adjectives by an accent mark.

MASCULINE	FEMININE	MEANING
éste	ésta	*this* (one)
éstos	éstas	*these*
ése	ésa	*that* (one)
ésos	ésas	*those*
aquél	aquélla	*that* (one)
aquéllos	aquéllas	*those*

este libro y aquél	*this book and that one*
estas plumas y ésas	*these pens and those*

EXERCISE F   **No estamos de acuerdo.** (We disagree.)   June and Cynthia are shopping for clothing but they rarely agree on anything. Complete their dialog with the appropriate forms of the demonstrative adjective and the demonstrative pronoun.

EXAMPLE: ¿Te gusta <u>este</u> traje de baño negro de aquí?   No, me gusta más <u>**ése**</u> de ahí.

1. ¿Te gustan _____ sandalias de allí?

   No, prefiero _____ de aquí.

2. ¿Te gusta _____ falda larga de ahí?

   Sí, pero prefiero _____ de allí.

3. ¿Te gusta _____ suéter blanco de aquí?

   No, me gusta más _____ anaranjado de ahí.

4. ¿Te gusta _____ vestido de allí?

   Sí, me gusta, pero prefiero _____ de ahí.

5. ¿Te gustan _____ zapatos rojos de aquí?

   No, prefiero _____ azules de ahí.

6. ¿Te gusta _____ sombrero de allí?

   No, me gusta más _____ de aquí.

7. ¿Te gustan _____ camisetas de ahí.

   Sí, pero prefiero _____ de allí.

8. ¿Te gusta _____ bolsa pequeña de aquí?

No, prefiero _____ de ahí.

EXERCISE G | **En el rastro** (At the flea market) Rogelio and a friend are at a flea market and are deciding what to buy. Complete their statements with the appropriate demonstrative adjective and demonstrative pronoun, based on the cues provided.

EXAMPLE: Voy a comprar **estos** discos compactos, no **aquéllos** (*de aquí / de allí*)

1. Prefiero _____ videojuego, no _____ . (*de allí / de ahí*)

2. Me gustan _____ videos, no _____ . (*de aquí / de ahí*)

3. _____ mochila es bonita, no me gusta _____ . (*de aquí / de allí*)

4. _____ camisetas son grandes, prefiero _____ . (*de aquí / de ahí*)

5. ¿Vas a comprar _____ zapatos de tenis o _____ ? (*de aquí / de allí*)

6. _____ revista es interesante pero prefiero _____ . (*de aquí / de ahí*)

7. Necesito una raqueta de tenis nueva. ¿Cuál te gusta más, _____ o _____ ?
(*de ahí / de allí*)

EXERCISE H | **De compras** You are shopping for school supplies with a friend with whom you usually disagree. Write a dialog of eight lines, using as many demonstrative adjectives and pronouns as possible.

_____

_____

_____

_____

_____

_____

_____

_____

CHAPTER 14
Possessive Adjectives

Possessive adjectives agree in gender (masculine or feminine) and number (singular or plural) with the person or thing possessed, not with the possessor.

SINGULAR	PLURAL	MEANING
mi hermano(-a)	mis hermanos(-as)	*my*
tu hermano(-a)	tus hermanos(-as)	*your* (sing. familiar)
su hermano(-a)	sus hermanos(-as)	*his, her, its, your* (sing. formal), *their*
nuestro(-a) hermano(-a)	nuestros(-as) hermanos(-as)	*our*
vuestro(-a) hermano(-a)	vuestros(-as) hermanos(-as)	*your* (fam. pl.)

su revista
$\begin{cases} \text{\textit{his, her, its magazine}} \\ \text{\textit{your magazine} (formal, sing. \& pl.)} \\ \text{\textit{their magazine}} \end{cases}$

sus revistas
$\begin{cases} \text{\textit{his, her, its magazines}} \\ \text{\textit{your} (formal, sing. \& pl.) \textit{magazines}} \\ \text{\textit{their magazines}} \end{cases}$

nuestra tía   *our aunt*
nuestras tías   *our aunts*

EXERCISE A | **La playa** You and some friends return from the beach and start to sort out the things you took with you. Use an appropriate possessive adjective to tell what belongs to whom.

EXAMPLE: las toallas / de Jaime   Son **sus** toallas.

1. las sandalias / de Yvonne _____

2. la pelota de voleibol / de Tomás _____

3. el aceite de broncear / de Virginia _____

4. los lentes de sol / Eduardo y de Tomás _____

5. la gorra / de Bernardo _____

6. el colchón de aire / de Felipe y Gustavo _____

7. el salvavidas / de Antonia _____

EXERCISE B   **El viaje ideal**   Johnny wrote a paragraph for school about his summer vacation. Complete it with the appropriate possessive adjectives.

Cada vez que _____ familia y yo regresamos de un viaje, _____ padres empiezan a
           1.   2.

hablar de _____ próximas vacaciones. Y por lo general, al día siguiente _____ padre
          3.   4.

le habla a _____ agente de viajes para planear _____ próximo viaje. _____ idea de
          5.   6.   7.

unas vacaciones perfectas es visitar otro país para conocer _____ costumbres y descansar
                                                        8.

en _____ playas. En el patio de _____ casa hay una piscina pero _____ padre
    9.   10.   11.

nunca nada en ella. Él prefiere la playa, con _____ arena suave y el mar azul,
                                           12.

con _____ suaves olas. _____ hermanos y yo compartimos _____ idea del viaje
     13.   14.   15.

perfecto y siempre tenemos _____ maletas listas para otro viaje fabuloso.
                             16.

EXERCISE C   **Acompañados**   Ramón is telling with whom he and his friends do different things. Express what he says.

EXAMPLE: yo / viajar / familia   Yo **viajo con mi** familia.

1. Elena / ir de compras / tía

   _____

2. Ralph y yo / jugar al fútbol / equipo

   _____

3. tú / jugar a los videojuegos / amigos

   _____

4. Janet / hablar / madre

   _____

5. Diane / bailar / novio

   _____

6. Gwen y Alba / pasar las vacaciones / primos

   _____

7. yo / comer / hermanos

   _____

8. Gabriel y yo / leer el periódico / abuela

   _____

EXERCISE D   **¿De quién es?** On the last day of camp, the counselors are cleaning up the playroom and want to know to whom different items belong. Answer their questions based on the cues provided. Use a possessive adjective in your response.

PARA EXPRESARSE MEJOR
Las posesiones

el monopatín *skateboard*   **el juego de damas** *checkers*
el videojuego *video game*   **el juego de ajedrez** *chess*
el cartel *poster*   **el guante de béisbol** *baseball glove*

EXAMPLE: ¿De quién es el guante de béisbol? (*Mario*)   Es **su** guante de béisbol.

1. ¿De quién es el fútbol? (*Ricardo*)

   _____

2. ¿De quién es el monopatín? (*tú*)

   _____

3. ¿De quién son los videojuegos? (*Antonio y yo*)

   _____

4. ¿De quién son los carteles? (*yo*)

   _____

5. ¿De quién son las fotos? (*Rebecca y Emma*)

   _____

6. ¿De quién es la raqueta de tenis? (*Andrea*)

   _____

7. ¿De quién es el juego de damas? (*Bill*)

   _____

8. ¿De quién son las pelotas de tenis? (*Francisco*)

   _____

9. ¿De quién es el juego de ajedrez? (*Nelson y yo*)

   _____

10. ¿De quién son los discos compactos? (*Sarita y Nilda*)

   _____

EXERCISE E   **Mi familia, mi casa y yo**   Write a paragraph of eight sentences in which you talk about your family, your house, and yourself. Use as many possessive adjectives as you can.

_____

_____

_____

_____

_____

_____

_____

_____

CHAPTER 15
The Preterit Tense of Regular Verbs

The preterit tense is used to express an action or event in the past. It may indicate the beginning or end of the action, or the complete action or event begun and finished in the past.

Beginning or End

María *comenzó* **a cantar.**	*María began to sing.*
Terminaron **el proyecto.**	*They finished the project.*

Complete Action

Hablé **con mi amiga anoche.**	*I spoke with my friend last night.*

1. Regular *-ar* Verbs

a. The preterit tense of regular *-ar* verbs is formed by dropping the infinitive ending *-ar* and adding the personal endings *-é, -aste, -ó, -amos, -asteis, -aron.*

	bailar to dance	contar to count
yo	bailé	conté
tú	bailaste	contaste
él, ella, Ud.	bailó	contó
nosotros, -as	bailamos	contamos
vosotros, -as	bailasteis	contasteis
ellos, ellas. Uds.	bailaron	contaron

b. In the preterit the *nosotros* ending (*-amos*) is the same as in the present tense: *hablamos* (we speak; we spoke).

c. Most verbs that are stem-changing (*o* to *ue; e* to *ie*) do not change the stem in the preterit tense: *contar: cuento* (present); *conté* (preterit).

d. The preterit tense has the following meanings in English:

tú *bailaste*	*you danced, you did dance*
él *contó*	*he counted / told*

e. Verbs that end in *-car, -gar,* and *-zar* have a spelling change in the *yo* form. In *-car* and *-gar* verbs, this change occurs to keep the original sound of the *c* and *g*. The change occurs in *-zar* verbs because *z* rarely precedes *e* or *i* in Spanish.

practi*car*	**yo practi***qué*
ju*gar*	**yo ju***gué*
comen*zar*	**yo comen***cé*

Other verbs that have these changes are:

-CAR	-GAR	-ZAR
buscar	llegar	almorzar
sacar	pagar	empezar
tocar		

f. Some expressions that are frequently used with the preterit are:

anoche	*last night*	**la semana pasada**	*last week*
ayer	*yesterday*	**el año pasado**	*last year*
anteayer	*the day before yesterday*	**el mes pasado**	*last month*

EXERCISE A   **La oficina de mi papá**   Susana is telling her parents what she observed when she and her sister spent the day at her father's office. Express what she says.

EXAMPLE: la secretaria / llegar tarde   La secretaria **llegó** tarde.

1. mi papá / trabajar con unos clientes

   _____

2. una señorita / pasar una hora en el teléfono

   _____

3. yo / contestar el teléfono una vez

   _____

4. Diana y yo / ayudar a los empleados

   _____

5. tú / firmar muchos contratos

   _____

6. algunos empleados / almorzar en su escritorio

   _____

7. todo el mundo / usar su computadora

   _____

8. la secretaria / dejar de trabajar a las cuatro y media

   _____

EXERCISE B   **Una fiesta de sorpresa**   Gina won a scholarship to study in Spain during the summer and her friends gave her a surprise party to celebrate the occasion. Tell what each person did.

EXAMPLE: Gina / ganar una beca   Gina **ganó** una beca.

1. yo / mandar las invitaciones

   _____

2. Andrea y Francisco / colgar los adornos

   _____

3. tú / preparar el pastel

   _____

4. Jackie / decorar el pastel

   _____

5. Vicki y yo / comprar el regalo

   _____

6. Antonia / arreglar la sala

   _____

7. Guy y Jorge / llevar los refrescos

   _____

8. todo el mundo / firmar la tarjeta

   _____

| EXERCISE C | **¿Dónde estás?**   Gloria is frantic because she can't get in touch with a friend by telephone. Complete the e-mail message she sent her with the appropriate form of the verbs in parentheses. |

Angela,

Cuando Nancy y yo _____ a casa anoche, yo _____ de llamarte
                    1. (regresar)   2. (tratar)

varias veces. Te _____ por los menos tres veces pero tú no _____ .
                  3. (llamar)   4. (contestar)

Yo _____ tres mensajes en tu máquina de contestar.
    5. (dejar)

    Anoche (ellos) _____ el concierto de tu cantante favorito en la televisión.
                              6. (pasar)

¿A qué hora _____ tú en la casa? ¿ _____ tú el concierto?
             7. (regresar)   8. (escuchar)

Hasta luego.

Estela

| EXERCISE D | **Después de las clases**   Tell what each person did after school yesterday. |

EXAMPLE: Ira / mirar la televisión   Ira **miró** la televisión.

1. Clarissa / practicar la flauta

_____

2. tú / escuchar discos compactos

_____

3. Edgardo / cuidar a su hermanito

_____

4. yo / terminar de leer una novela

_____

5. Fran y Luisa / estudiar para un examen

_____

6. María / caminar por el parque

_____

7. Jerry y yo / cortar el césped

_____

8. Carol / comenzar un curso de conducir

_____

EXERCISE E   **Una nota**   Use the appropriate form of the verbs in parentheses to complete the note that Tomás wrote to a friend.

Querido David:

La semana pasada yo _____ en un restaurante con un amigo. Yo
                        1. (almorzar)

_____ temprano y _____ a hablar español con el mesero. Al salir
   2. (llegar)   3. (empezar)

del restaurante yo _____ mi dinero pero no lo _____ .
                      4. (buscar)   5. (encontrar)

Yo _____ una tarjeta de crédito y _____ la cuenta con ella. Al
      6. (sacar)   7. (pagar)

llegar a casa yo _____ a un videojuego.
                    8. (jugar)

Hasta luego.

Tomás

2.   Regular -ER and -IR Verbs

a. The preterit tense of regular -er and -ir verbs is formed by dropping the infinitive ending -er or -ir and adding the personal endings -í, -iste, -ió, -imos, -isteis, -ieron.

	comer to eat	vivir to live
yo	comí	viví
tú	comiste	viviste
él, ella, Ud.	comió	vivió
nosotros, -as	comimos	vivimos
vosotros, -as	comisteis	vivisteis
ellos, ellas. Uds.	comieron	vivieron

b. The preterit endings are the same for -er and -ir verbs.

c. In -ir verbs, the *nosotros* ending (-imos) is the same as in the present tense. In -er verbs, the endings are different.

abrimos	*we open*	**abrimos**	*we opened*
perdemos	*we lose*	**perdimos**	*we lost*

d. The accent mark is omitted over the following forms of *ver: vi, vio.*

e. Stem-changing verbs ending in -er do not change the stem vowel in the preterit tense. Stem-changing verbs ending in -ir have special stem changes in the preterit and are not discussed here.

EXERCISE F   **Decisiones**   After your first day back at school, you tell a friend what several of your classmates decided to do during the summer vacation.

EXAMPLE: Jim / tomar un curso avanzado   Jim **decidió** tomar un curso avanzado.

1. Pedro y Enrique / hacer un viaje

   _____

2. tú / ir a la playa todos los días

   _____

3. Efraín / ayudar a su padre

   _____

4. Gisela y yo / leer muchas novelas

   _____

5. Lisa / aprender otro idioma

   _____

6. Mickey y Carlos / trabajar en la oficina de un veterinario

   _____

7. yo / descansar lo más posible

   _____

8. Arlene / dominar la computadora

_____

EXERCISE G **Un viaje divertido** Paul was the official photographer on the class trip to Washington. Tell what the person in each picture did during the trip. Use *sacar, ver, comprar, escribir, descubrir,* and *conocer* in your answers.

PARA EXPRESARSE MEJOR

Una visita a la capital.

la obra de arte *a work of art*   **el monumento** *monument*

el recuerdo *souvenir*   **senador(-ora)** *senator*

la tarjeta postal *postcard*

EXAMPLE: Los alumnos **visitaron los monumentos**.

1. Susan y Linda _____

_____ .

3. Tú _____

_____ .

2. Migdalia y yo _____

_____ .

4. Mis amigos _____

_____ .

5. Manuel _____

_____.

6. Yo _____

_____.

| EXERCISE H | **Muchas preguntas** Henry's mother is always asking him many questions. Answer her questions using the cues provided. |

1. ¿Pasaste un buen rato en la escuela hoy? (*sí*)

   _____

2. ¿Quién te acompañó a la casa? (*John y Fred*)

   _____

3. ¿Cómo saliste en el examen de matemáticas? (*mal*)

   _____

4. ¿Cuántas horas estudiaste para el examen? (*dos*)

   _____

5. ¿A qué hora volvieron Uds. de la excursión al acuario? (*2:30*)

   _____

6. ¿Sacaste tus cosas de la mochila? (*no*)

   _____

7. ¿Conociste a la nueva directora de la escuela hoy? (*no*)

   _____

8. ¿Cuándo hablaste con tu primo? (*anoche*)

   _____

9. ¿Cuándo regresó él de su viaje? (*el domingo pasado*)

   _____

10. ¿Cuándo practicaste el piano? (*ayer*)

    _____

11. ¿Cuándo jugaste al tenis? (*anteayer*)

    _____

12. ¿Qué decidiste hacer esta noche? (*ver un video*)

    _____

EXERCISE I   **Alternativas**   Use the cues provided to tell what you did in the following situations.

EXAMPLE: El ascensor del edificio no funcionó.   (*salir del ascensor y subir por la escalera*)
   Salí del ascensor y **subí** por la escalera.

1. Perdiste las llaves.   (*buscarlas en todas partes*)

   _____

2. El número de teléfono que marcaste está ocupado.   (*marcarlo otra vez*)

   _____

3. No tienen el video que quieres en la tienda de videos.   (*sacar otro video*)

   _____

4. Tu amiga Gloria no juega al tenis.   (*jugar a otro deporte*)

   _____

5. No te gustó el plato que pediste en el restaurante.   (*devolverlo y pedir otra cosa*)

   _____

6. En el cine no hay boletos para la función de las cinco.   (*esperar la próxima función*)

   _____

7. No te quedó dinero para subir al autobús.   (*caminar a casa*)

   _____

8. Viste a un amigo en el centro.   (*saludarlo e invitarle a tomar un refresco*)

   _____

EXERCISE J   **Actividades**   Tell who did the following activities last night.

yo	perder las llaves
mi padre	ver la televisión
mi madre	aprender un poema de memoria
mis hermanos	jugar al boliche
tú	sacar dinero del banco
mis padres	estudiar para un examen
un amigo	buscar un juego
mi hermana y yo	asistir a una clase de ejercicio
	participar en un concurso
	practicar un deporte

1. _____

2. _____

3. _____

4. _____

5. _____

6. _____

7. _____

8. _____

9. _____

10. _____

EXERCISE K   **Las vacaciones del año pasado**   Write a paragraph of eight sentences in which you describe the things you did while on vacation last year.

_____

_____

_____

_____

_____

_____

_____

CHAPTER 16
Commands

1. Formal Commands of Regular Verbs

a. Formal commands are formed by dropping the final -*o* from the *yo* form of the present tense and adding the following:

	-AR	-ER	-IR
Ud.	-e	-a	-a
Uds.	-en	-an	-an

INFINITIVE	PRESENT TENSE YO FORM	COMMAND FORMS SINGULAR	PLURAL	MEANING
cerrar	cierro	cierre	cierren	close
tomar	tomo	tome	tomen	take
comer	como	coma	coman	eat
hacer	hago	haga	hagan	do, make
leer	leo	lea	lean	read
perder	pierdo	pierda	pierdan	lose
tener	tengo	tenga	tengan	have
ver	veo	vea	vean	see
volver	vuelvo	vuelva	vuelvan	return
decir	digo	diga	digan	say, tell
servir	sirvo	sirva	sirvan	serve
traducir	traduzco	traduzca	traduzcan	translate
venir	vengo	venga	vengan	come

b. The negative command is formed by placing *no* before the verb.

No trabajen mucho.	*Don't work a lot.*
No lea en voz alta.	*Don't read aloud.*

c. Verbs ending in -*zar*, -*car*, and -*gar* have spelling changes in the command forms. The changes in -*zar* verbs occur because in Spanish, *z* is rarely followed by *e* or *i*. The changes in -*car* and -*gar* verbs occur to preserve the original sounds of *c* and *g*.

INFINITIVE	PRESENT TENSE YO FORM	COMMAND FORMS SINGULAR	PLURAL	MEANING
comenzar	comienzo	comience	comiencen	begin
practicar	practico	practique	practiquen	practice
jugar	juego	juegue	jueguen	play

EXERCISE A **La sala de espera** While Javier waits his turn in the doctor's office, the receptionist tells him to do different things. Express what the receptionist says.

EXAMPLE: tomar asiento **Tome** asiento.

1. llenar el formulario _____

2. escribir claramente _____

3. contestar todas las preguntas _____

4. leer una revista _____

5. poner el abrigo en el armario _____

6. tener paciencia _____

7. no hablar en voz muy alta _____

8. hacer otra cita _____

EXERCISE B **El médico recomienda** Mr. Sandoval isn't feeling very well and visits the doctor. Express what the doctor tells him to do.

EXAMPLE: comprar la medicina **Compre** la medicina.

1. beber muchos líquidos

_____

2. guardar cama por dos días

_____

3. descansar mucho

_____

4. comenzar a tomar la medicina en seguida

_____

5. comer muchas frutas y verduras

_____

6. dormir por lo menos ocho horas

_____

7. no practicar ningún deporte

_____

8. volver en una semana

_____

EXERCISE C   **Un paseo en carro**   The Torres family is taking a car trip. Express the commands that Mr. and Mrs. Torres give to their children.

EXAMPLE: mirar por la ventana   **Miren** por la ventana.
           no abrir la ventana   **No abran** la ventana.

1. contar los carros rojos   _____

2. leer las revistas   _____

3. hacer el rompecabezas   _____

4. no pelear   _____

5. beber los refrescos   _____

6. no comer los dulces   _____

7. no gritar   _____

8. no poner los pies en la silla   _____

9. cerrar los ojos   _____

10. no cantar esa canción   _____

EXERCISE D   **El cliente siempre tiene la razón.**   Hilda is working in a department store for the holidays. Express what her supervisor tells her she must do.

EXAMPLE: atender bien a los clientes   ¡**Atienda** bien a los clientes!

1. empezar a trabajar en seguida   _____

2. no perder tiempo   _____

3. ofrecer su ayuda   _____

4. mostrar muchas cosas al cliente   _____

5. pedir lo que quieren ver   _____

6. buscar lo que quieren ver   _____

7. recordar lo que pide el cliente   _____

8. volver en seguida con la mercancía   _____

9. resolver cualquier problema   _____

10. cerrar la caja con cuidado   _____

EXERCISE E   **Las reglas** (Rules)   Mrs. Gutiérrez is explaining rules of behavior to her kindergarten students. Express what she says as commands.

EXAMPLE: Los niños deben hablar en voz baja.
           Hablen en voz baja.

1. Los niños deben caminar en el patio.

   _____

2. Los niños deben compartir los juguetes.

   _____

3. Los niños deben respetar a los otros niños.

   _____

4. Los niños deben meter las mochilas debajo de sus pupitres.

   _____

5. Los niños deben esperar su turno para hablar.

   _____

6. Los niños deben pedir permiso a la maestra.

   _____

7. Los niños no deben hacer bromas.

   _____

8. Los niños deben seguir las reglas.

   _____

2. Formal Commands of Irregular Verbs

The following verbs have irregular formal command forms:

INFINITIVE	PRESENT TENSE YO FORM	COMMAND FORMS SINGULAR	PLURAL	MEANING
dar	doy	dé	den	give
estar	estoy	esté	estén	be
ir	voy	vaya	vayan	go
ser	soy	sea	sean	be

NOTE: 1. _Dé_ has an accent mark to distinguish it from _de_ (of).

2. _Esté_ and _estén_ have accent marks to indicate that the stress falls on the last syllable.

EXERCISE F **La responsabilidad** David's father is always telling him and his brother how to be responsible young adults. Express what he tells them to do.

EXAMPLE: hablar cortésmente **Hablen** cortésmente.

1. dar la mano _____

2. estar a tiempo _____

3. ir con cuidado _____

4. ser amables _____

5. decir la verdad _____

6. no presumir _____

3. Commands with Object Pronouns

a. Direct and indirect object pronouns follow affirmative commands and are attached to them. A written accent mark is usually required on the vowel that is stressed.

Há*galo* ahora.	*Do it now.*
Escríban*me* pronto.	*Write to me soon.*
Préste*les* el dinero.	*Lend them the money.*

b. In negative commands, the object pronoun precedes the verb.

No *lo* haga ahora.	*Don't do it now.*
No *me* escriban pronto.	*Don't write to me soon.*
No *les* preste el dinero.	*Don't lend them the money.*

EXERCISE G | **Háganlo así** The teacher is telling the students what they should do. Express what she says.

EXAMPLE: abrir el libro y leerlo   **Abran** el libro y **léanlo**.

1. hacer la tarea y entregarla

_____

2. escuchar las frases y repetirlas

_____

3. estudiar esta lección y aprenderla

_____

4. comprar los útiles y usarlos

_____

5. ver el párrafo y copiarlo

_____

6. leer la palabra y escribirla

_____

7. traer los libros a la clase y usarlos en la clase

_____

8. mirar los exámenes y revisarlos

_____

| **EXERCISE H** | **En el restaurante** Nelson likes to take charge when he and friends eat in a restaurant. Express what he tells the waiter using the appropriate indirect object pronoun. |

EXAMPLE: traer el menú / a nosotros   **Tráiganos** el menú.

1. servir la sopa ahora / a mí   _____

2. buscar otro tenedor / a él   _____

3. decir las especialidades del día / a nosotros _____

4. quitar el plato sucio / a ella   _____

5. dar la cuenta / a ellos   _____

4.   Affirmative Familiar Commands (Singular)

a. The affirmative *tú* command of regular verbs and stem-changing verbs is the same as the *Ud.* form of the present tense.

INFINITIVE	TÚ COMMAND (PRESENT TENSE, UD. FORM)	MEANING
cerrar	cierra	close
comer	come	eat
dar	da	give
leer	lee	read
perder	pierde	lose
servir	sirve	serve
tomar	toma	take
ver	ve	see
volver	vuelve	return

b. The following verbs have irregular affirmative *tú* commands:

INFINITIVE	COMMAND TÚ FORM	MEANING
decir	di	say, tell
hacer	haz	do, make
ir	ve	go
poner	pon	put
salir	sal	leave, go out
ser	sé	be
tener	ten	have
venir	ven	come

NOTE: 1. Subject pronouns are usually omitted.

2. The familiar commands are used: between friends and classmates; by parents and other adults when speaking to young children; and in other cases where there is a familiar (not a formal) relationship.

EXERCISE I **Te toca a ti.** (It's your turn.)   Everyone in the Medina family helps with the household chores. Tell what Mrs. Medina says as she assigns the different chores.

PARA EXPRESARSE MEJOR
Los quehaceres domésticos

lavar *to wash*

pasar la aspiradora *to vacuum*

sacudir los muebles *to dust*

barrer *to sweep*

sacar la basura *to take out the garbage*

limpiar *to clean*

EXAMPLE: Rosa, **lava la ropa**.

1. Felipe, _____

_____ .

3. Anita, _____

_____ .

2. Arturo, _____

_____ .

4. Felipe, _____

_____ .

5. Rosa, _____   6. Arturo, _____

_____ .   _____ .

| **EXERCISE J** | **Están en su casa.** When Beto's friends come to his house, he tries to make them feel at home and tells each one what to do. Express what he tells them. |

EXAMPLE: Tengo sed. (*pedir un refresco*)   **Pide** un refresco.

1. Quiero saber el tanteo del partido de fútbol. (*escuchar el noticiero*)

_____

2. Tengo hambre. (*comer un sándwich*)

_____

3. Quiero leer pero está oscuro. (*encender la luz*)

_____

4. ¿Qué hora es? (*mirar ese reloj*)

_____

5. Quiero jugar al béisbol con tu hermano. (*usar mi guante*)

_____

5. Negative Familiar Commands (Singular)

a. To form a negative *tú* command, use the stem of the *yo* form of the present tense and add *-es* for *-ar* verbs and *-as* for *-er* and *-ir* verbs.

INFINITIVE	PRESENT TENSE YO FORM	NEGATIVE FAMILIAR COMMAND	MEANING
abrir	abro	no abras	*don't open*
cerrar	cierro	no cierres	*don't close*
decir	digo	no digas	*don't say, tell*
leer	leo	no leas	*don't read*
perder	pierdo	no pierdas	*don't lose*
servir	sirvo	no sirvas	*don't serve*
tener	tengo	no tengas	*don't have*
tomar	tomo	no tomes	*don't take*
ver	veo	no veas	*don't see*

b. The following verbs have irregular *tú* commands:

INFINITIVE	NEGATIVE TÚ COMMAND	MEANING
decir	di	*say, tell*
hacer	haz	*do, make*
ir	ve	*go*
poner	pon	*put*
salir	sal	*leave, go out*
ser	sé	*be*
tener	ten	*have*
venir	ven	*come*

c. Verbs that end in *-zar, -car,* and *-gar* have spelling changes in the negative command forms. The spelling change in *-zar* verbs occurs because in Spanish, *z* is rarely followed by *e* or *i.* The spelling change in *-car* and *-gar* verbs occurs to preserve the original sounds of *c* and *g.*

INFINITIVE	PRESENT TENSE YO FORM	NEGATIVE TÚ COMMAND	MEANING
almorzar	almuerzo	no almuerces	*don't have lunch*
tocar	toco	no toques	*don't touch, play*
pagar	pago	no pagues	*don't pay*

EXERCISE K | **En el parque** While in the park, you hear a mother telling her child not to do several things. Express what the mother says.

EXAMPLE: no hablarle a nadie   ¡No le **hables** a nadie!

1. no tocar las flores   _____

2. no ir lejos   _____

3. no saludar a las personas   _____

4. no dejar la pelota allí   _____

5. no hacer eso   _____

6. no ponerte los dedos sucios en la boca   _____

7. no gritar   _____

8. no perder la gorra   _____

9. no correr tan rápido   _____

10. no tener miedo de los perros   _____

EXERCISE L   **Escúchame.** (Listen to me.)   It seems to Fred that his mother is always telling him what to do and what not to do. Express what his mother tells him.

EXAMPLE: hacer la tarea ahora / no dejarla para más tarde
          Haz la tarea ahora; no **la dejes** para más tarde.

1. guardar los libros / no ponerlos en la mesa del comedor

   _____

2. usar los tenis / no salir a jugar en esos zapatos

   _____

3. venir con nosotros al centro comercial / no mirar la televisión

   _____

4. poner la botella vacía en la basura / no meterla en el refrigerador

   _____

5. ayudar a tu padre / no llamar a tus amigos por teléfono

   _____

6. cerrar la puerta bien / no cerrarla tan fuertemente

   _____

7. descansar después del partido / no comenzar a jugar otro partido

   _____

EXERCISE M   **Problemas y soluciones**   Tell some friends what they should do to solve the problems they present to you. Use the solution given in parentheses and an object pronoun, when appropriate.

EXAMPLE: Tengo resfriado.   (*beber mucho jugo*)
          Bebe mucho jugo.

          Tengo que hacer la tarea.   (*hacer la tarea pronto*)
          Hazla pronto.

1. Toda mi ropa está sucia.   (*lavar la ropa*)

   _____

2. Me duele la cabeza.   (*tomar dos aspirinas*)

   _____

3. Tengo dolor de muelas.   (*hacer una cita con el dentista*)

   _____

4. Tengo mucha tarea de la clase de inglés.   (*comenzar la tarea ahora*)

   _____

5. Tengo mucha hambre. (*ir a la cafetería*)

_____

6. No comprendo la lección de matemáticas. (*pedir ayuda al maestro*)

_____

7. Me duele el estómago. (*no comer nada*)

_____

EXERCISE N   ¡Conserven energía! Prepare two lists of eight *Uds.*-commands that tell people how to protect the environment. The first list should contain eight commands of what they should do; the second one, eight commands indicating what they should not do.

PARA EXPRESARSE MEJOR
El medio ambiente   *(The environment)*

apagar *to shut off*	**la basura** *garbage*
encender *to light (a fire)*	**el transporte público** *public transportation*
separar *to separate*	**los árboles** *trees*
reciclar *to recycle*	**el aire** *air*
proteger *to protect*	**los periódicos** *newspapers*
cortar *to cut*	**el bosque** *forest*
contaminar *to contaminate*	**el fuego** *fire*

_____	_____
_____	_____
_____	_____
_____	_____
_____	_____
_____	_____

CHAPTER 17
Negation

1. Principal Negatives and Their Opposite Affirmatives

NEGATIVE		AFFIRMATIVE	
no	*no, not*	**sí**	*yes*
nadie	*no one, nobody, (not) anyone*	**alguien**	*someone, somebody, anyone*
nada	*nothing, (not) anything*	**algo**	*something, anything*
nunca **jamás**	*never (not) ever*	**siempre**	*always*
tampoco	*neither, not either*	**también**	*also*
ninguno(-a)	*no, none, (not) any*	**alguno(-a)**	*some, any*
ni... ni	*neither . . . nor, not . . . nor*	**o... o**	*either . . . or*

a. The most common negative is *no*, which always precedes the conjugated verb.

> **Ella *no* va al teatro.**   *She is not going to the theater.*
> **¿*No* trabajas hoy?** *Aren't you working today?*

b. Double negatives are acceptable in Spanish and occur frequently. If one of the negatives is *no*, it precedes the verb. If *no* is omitted, the other negative must precede the verb.

> **Ellos *no* cantan nunca.** ⎫
> **Ellos *nunca* cantan.** ⎭ *They never sing.*

c. *Nadie* can be used as the subject or the object of the verb. When it is the object of the verb, it is preceded by the preposition *a*.

> ***Nadie* juega.** ⎫
> **No juega *nadie*.** ⎭ *No one plays.*

BUT:

> **No le hablo *a nadie*.** ⎫
> ***A nadie* le hablo.** ⎭ *I don't speak to anyone.*

d. *Ninguno* drops the final *-o* and requires a written accent over the *u* if it immediately precedes a masculine singular noun. If a preposition comes between *ninguno* and the noun, the full form is used.

> ***Ningún* libro es interesante.**   *No book is interesting.*
> ***Ninguno* de los libros es interesante.**   *None of the books is interesting.*
> ***Ninguna* revista es interesante.**   *No magazine is interesting.*

e. Like *ninguno, alguno* drops the final *-o* and requires a written accent over the *u* if it comes immediately before a masculine singular noun. If a preposition comes between *alguno* and the noun, the full form is used.

Algún **baile es divertido.**   *Some dance is enjoyable.*

Alguno **de los bailes es divertido.**   *Some of the dances are enjoyable.*

EXERCISE A   **¡No, no, no!**   Erica is not cooperating with her babysitter. Express what she answers in response to the suggestions her babysitter makes.

EXAMPLE: Debes guardar los juguetes.   **No guardo** los juguetes.

1. Debes descansar ahora. _____

2. Debes comer las galletas. _____

3. Debes buscar los zapatos. _____

4. Debes hablar en voz baja. _____

5. Debes poner el vaso en la cocina. _____

6. Debes recoger los libros. _____

7. Debes dormir la siesta. _____

EXERCISE B   **¿Qué vas a hacer esta noche?**   A friend wants to know your plans for tonight but you don't have any. Answer your friend's questions.

EXAMPLE: ¿Vas a escuchar música esta noche?   **No, no voy** a escuchar **nada** esta noche.

1. ¿Vas a comer algo esta noche?

_____

2. ¿Vas a ver algo en la televisión esta noche?

_____

3. ¿Vas a beber algo esta noche?

_____

4. ¿Vas a comprar algo esta noche?

_____

5. ¿Vas a jugar videojuegos esta noche?

_____

6. ¿Vas a dibujar algo esta noche?

_____

7. ¿Vas a leer algo esta noche?

_____

EXERCISE C | **¿Quién va a traer... ?**   The Spanish Club is planning a beach party. The president wants to know what everyone will bring but no one is planning to bring anything. Express the president's comments after she asks the questions.

EXAMPLE: ¿Quién va a traer una pelota de voleibol a la playa?
Nadie va a traer una pelota de voleibol a la playa.

1. ¿Quién va a traer los refrescos a la playa?

   _____

2. ¿Quién va a traer las toallas a la playa?

   _____

3. ¿Quién va a traer el aceite de broncear a la playa?

   _____

4. ¿Quién va a traer los sándwiches a la playa?

   _____

5. ¿Quién va a traer los dulces a la playa?

   _____

6. ¿Quién va a traer los juegos de mesa a la playa?

   _____

EXERCISE D | **Ellos nunca hacen eso.**   Tell what some of your friends never do.

EXAMPLE: Mónica / montar en bicicleta
Mónica **nunca monta** en bicicleta.   OR: Mónica **no monta nunca** en bicicleta.

1. Jacques / esquiar en las montañas

   _____

2. Orlando y yo / jugar videojuegos

   _____

3. yo / mandar tarjetas de cumpleaños

   _____

4. Claudio y Enrique / asistir a un concierto

   _____

5. tú / darles regalos a los amigos

   _____

6. Sarita / visitar a los amigos

   _____

EXERCISE E ¿**Quiénes no hacen eso?** You are discussing what some friends do and want to know if others do the same thing. Tell what these friends don't do, using the opposite of the underlined word.

EXAMPLE: Estela <u>siempre</u> saca fotos en las fiestas. ¿Y Victoria?
Victoria **nunca** saca fotos en las fiestas.

1. Jessie <u>siempre</u> va de compras con <u>alguien</u>. ¿Y tú?

   _____

2. Yo le hablo a <u>alguien</u> por teléfono cada tarde. ¿Y Andrea?

   _____

3. Norma compra <u>algo</u> cuando va de compras. ¿Y Valerie?

   _____

4. Nosotros siempre estudiamos con <u>alguien</u>. ¿Y Luis y Ricky?

   _____

5. Gladys canta con <u>alguien</u> en la fiesta. ¿Y Uds.?

   _____

6. Tina <u>siempre</u> me pide <u>algo</u>. ¿Y Alison?

   _____

EXERCISE F **No lo hacen.** Tell what the following people don't do.

EXAMPLE: ver la televisión / leer una revista / Esteban
Esteban **no ve** la televisión **ni lee** una revista.

1. comer dulces / hacer ejercicio / Antonia

   _____

2. jugar al tenis / nadar / Laura y Nancy

   _____

3. ayudar en casa / practicar el piano / Clara

   _____

4. aceptar regalos / comprar regalos / David

   _____

5. hablarle a su hermano / salir con él / Efraín

   _____

EXERCISE G **Ni yo tampoco.** Jorge and a new friend find that they have many similar habits. Express what Jorge says.

EXAMPLE: EL AMIGO: A mí no me gusta el pescado.

JORGE: A mí no me gusta el pescado **tampoco**.

1. EL AMIGO: Yo nunca voy a la biblioteca.

   JORGE: _____

2. EL AMIGO: Yo no toco ningún instrumento musical.

   JORGE: _____

3. EL AMIGO: No me gusta ayudar en casa.

   JORGE: _____

4. EL AMIGO: No me gustan las películas románticas.

   JORGE: _____

5. EL AMIGO: Yo nunca visito a mis primos.

   JORGE: _____

EXERCISE H   **Regalos**   Nora wants to buy a gift for a young cousin. Her mother tells her that the cousin doesn't need what she suggests. Express what the mother says.

EXAMPLE: un suéter   **No, no necesita ningún** suéter.

1. una muñeca   _____

2. un juguete   _____

3. marcadoras   _____

4. un rompecabezas   _____

5. un animal de peluche   _____

6. patines   _____

EXERCISE I   **La soledad** (Loneliness)   Alfredo is going to camp for the first time and is nervous about the experience. Using the appropriate negative expressions, complete the description of one of his experiences.

Al subir en el autobús, me doy cuenta de que yo _____ conozco _____ .
                                                    1.   2.

Tomo un asiento donde _____ está sentado. Miro las caras de los otros chicos
                          3.

en el autobús pero _____ reconozco _____ cara. _____ chico
                       4.   5.   6.

decide sentarse conmigo. _____ puedo entretenerme durante el viaje porque
                              7.

_____ tengo _____ un libro _____ un juego electrónico
      8.   9.   10.

en mi mochila. _____ trata de saludarme y yo _____ saludo
                        11.   12.

_____ _____ .
        13.   14.

Estoy nervioso y pienso que _____ voy a ir a un campamento donde
                                        15.

_____ conozco a _____ persona.
        16.   17.

2. Frequently Used Negative Expressions

Creo que *no*.	*I don't think so.*
De *nada*.	*You're welcome.* (answer to **Gracias**)
en *ningún* lado **en *ninguna* parte**	*nowhere*
***Ni* yo *tampoco*.**	*Me neither.*
***No* es así.**	*It's not so.*
***No* es para tanto.**	*It's not such a big deal.*
***No* hay más remedio.**	*It can't be helped.*
***No* importa.**	*It doesn't matter.*
***No* lo creo.**	*I don't believe it.*
¡*No* me digas!	*Don't tell me!* (*You don't say!*)
***No* me gusta nada.**	*I don't like it at all.*
***No* puede ser.**	*It can't be.*
***No* puedo más.**	*I can't take any more.*
¿ *No* te parece?	*Don't you think so?*
¿Por qué *no*?	*Why not?*

EXERCISE J   **Reacciones**   Use one of the following expressions to react to a friend's statements or questions.

De nada.	**No lo creo.**	**No me gusta nada.**
En ninguna parte.	**¡No me digas!**	**¿No te parece?**
No hay más remedio.	**No es para tanto.**	**¿Por qué no?**
Ni yo tampoco.	**No puedo más.**	

EXAMPLE: AMIGO: ¿Dónde venden ese juego electrónico?

        TÚ: **En ninguna parte.**

1. AMIGO: Vicente y yo vamos a ir al cine tres veces esta semana.

     TÚ: _____

2. AMIGO: Alex recibió un carro de último modelo cuando se graduó.

     TÚ: _____

3. AMIGO: Yo no pienso trabajar durante el verano.

    TÚ: _____

4. AMIGO: Elsa y yo comimos en un restaurante japonés anoche.

    TÚ: _____

5. AMIGO: Annie está saliendo con Carlos otra vez.

    TÚ: _____

6. AMIGO: La mamá de Celia está enferma y Celia tiene que ayudar en casa.

    TÚ: _____

7. AMIGO: Debemos tener una fiesta para celebrar el comienzo de las vacaciones.

    TÚ: _____

8. AMIGO: Tú peleas con tus hermanas todos los días.

    TÚ: _____

9. AMIGO: Muchas gracias por tu ayuda.

    TÚ: _____

10. AMIGO: Clarisa lleva ropa muy elegante.

    TÚ: Gasta mucho dinero en su ropa, _____

EXERCISE K   **¡No puede ser!**   Write a letter of ten sentences to a friend. In it, describe a series of events in which nothing turned out the way it should have. Use as many negative expressions in your letter as possible.

_____

_____

_____

_____

_____

_____

_____

_____

CHAPTER 18
SABER and *CONOCER*; Idiomatic Verbal Expressions

1. *SABER* and *CONOCER*

a. *Saber* and *conocer* both mean "to know." However, they are used in different contexts or situations. All of the present tense forms of these two verbs are regular except the *yo* form.

	saber	conocer
yo	sé	conozco
tú	sabes	conoces
él, ella, Ud.	sabe	conoce
nosotros, -as	sabemos	conocemos
vosotros, -as	sabéis	conocéis
ellos, ellas. Uds.	saben	conocen

b. *Saber* means "to know a fact, to have information about something, to know how to do something." *Saber* can be followed by a noun, a clause, or an infinitive.

Ella *sabe* mi dirección.	*She knows my address.*
Yo *sé* dónde ella trabaja.	*I know where she works.*
Ellos *no saben* patinar.	*They don't know how to skate.*

c. *Conocer* means "to know personally, to be acquainted with, to be familiar with." *Conocer* can be followed by names of people, places, or things.

***Conozco* a la señora Vidal.**	*I know Mrs. Vidal.*
Él *conoce* Madrid.	*He knows Madrid.*
Ellas *conocen* una playa bonita.	*They are familiar with a beautiful beach.*

d. Note the difference in meaning between the following sentences:

Ella *sabe* el nombre del doctor.	*She knows the doctor's name.*
Ella *conoce* al doctor.	*She knows the doctor.*

EXERCISE A   ¿Sabes...? Based on the drawings, tell what each person knows or knows how to do.

EXAMPLE: Sammy **sabe conducir un carro**.

1. Victor y yo _____

   _____ .

2. Amy _____

   _____ .

3. Tú _____

   _____ .

4. Yo _____

   _____ .

5. Alfredo _____

   _____ .

6. Frances _____

   _____ .

| EXERCISE B |

Saben mucho.   Tammy is taking care of some younger cousins and has told them some facts about herself. Now she wants to see what they know. Express what the younger cousins say in response to her statements.

EXAMPLE: TAMMY: Me llamo Tammy.

ALICIA: **Yo sé cómo te llamas. / Yo sé tu nombre**.

1. TAMMY: Yo tengo dieciséis años.

   JENNY Y YO: _____

2. TAMMY: Vivo en la Calle Lerma, 234.

   PAUL: _____

3. TAMMY: Estudio en la Escuela Secundaria Kennedy.

   ENRIQUE: _____

4. TAMMY: Tengo el pelo rubio.

   DORIS: _____

5. TAMMY: Vivo con mis padres y mis dos hermanas.

   RICKY Y YO: _____

6. TAMMY: Mi comida favorita es la ensalada.

   SARITA: _____

7. TAMMY: Me fascina jugar al voleibol.

   SARITA Y YO: _____

8. TAMMY: Yo nací el 15 de diciembre.

   DORIS: _____

EXERCISE C   **¡A Madrid!**   Phil joins a student tour to Madrid and is getting to know the others in the group. They have all been to Madrid before and tell the places they already know. Express what they say.

EXAMPLE: Johnny / el Palacio Real   Johnny **conoce** el Palacio Real.

1. yo / varios restaurantes buenos   _____

2. Estela / el Parque del Buen Retiro   _____

3. José / una discoteca popular   _____

4. Manny y yo / la Puerta del Sol   _____

5. tú / el metro de Madrid   _____

6. Sofía / unas tiendas interesantes   _____

7. Sue y Erica / el Museo del Prado   _____

8. yo / un café divertido   _____

EXERCISE D   **Planes**   Helen and June are going to spend the day together and talk about their plans. Complete the dialog below with the appropriate forms of *saber* or *conocer*.

HELEN: ¿ _____ (tú) lo que quiero hacer hoy?
                        1.

JUNE: Yo nunca _____ en que estás pensando.
                          2.

HELEN: Quiero _____ el nuevo salón del museo donde hay una exposición de
                        3.
   las obras de Picasso.

JUNE: Está bien, pero yo no _____ nada de su arte.
                                4.

HELEN: No importa. En el museo hay guías que _____ mucho y te acompañan
                                                      5.
   y explican cada pintura.

JUNE: ¿ _____ a qué hora abren la exposición?
                          6.

HELEN: Podemos llamar por teléfono para _____ la hora.
                                                        7.

JUNE: Y después de visitar el museo podemos ir a comer. Yo _____ un buen
                                                                              8.
        restaurante español.

HELEN: Tú siempre _____ los mejores restaurantes. ¿ _____
                           9.   10.
        cuánto cuesta la comida? Yo no _____ si tengo bastante dinero.
                                              11.

JUNE: Yo no _____ , pero si es caro yo _____ otros restaurantes
                     12.   13.
        más económicos.

HELEN: Vamos. Quiero _____ los lugares que tú recomiendas.
                              14.

2.   Idiomatic Verbal Expressions

Many Spanish verbs are used in idiomatic expressions. (Idiomatic expressions with *tener* appear in Chapter 11.)

a. Expressions with *HACER*

¿Qué tiempo *hace*?	*How's the weather?*
¿Qué tiempo *hace* en la Florida?	*How's the weather in Florida?*
hacer **buen / mal tiempo**	*to be good (bad) weather*
Hace **mucho calor.**	*It's very hot.*
hacer **(mucho) frío / calor / fresco**	*to be (very) cold / warm / cool (weather)*
Hace **mucho frío.**	*It's very cold.*
hacer **(mucho) sol**	*to be (very) sunny*
Hace **mucho sol a mediodía.**	*It's very sunny at noon.*
hacer **(mucho) viento**	*to be (very) windy*
Hace **viento por la tarde.**	*It's windy in the afternoon.*
hacer **el favor de** + infinitive	*please . . .*
Haga **el favor de llamarme.**	*Please call me.*
hacer **un viaje**	*to take a trip*
Hace **un viaje cada verano.**	*He takes a trip each summer.*
hacer **una pregunta**	*to ask a question*
Ellos *hacen* muchas preguntas.	*They ask many questions.*
hacer **una visita**	*to pay a visit*
Ellos *hacen* una visita a sus primos.	*They pay a visit to their cousins.*

EXERCISE E   **El mapa del tiempo**   Using the weather map below, tell what the weather is the cities indicated.

EXAMPLE: ¿Qué tiempo hace en Dallas?   **Hace buen tiempo** en Dallas.

1. ¿Qué tiempo hace en Denver? _____

2. ¿Qué tiempo hace en San Francisco? _____

3. ¿Qué tiempo hace en Atlanta? _____

4. ¿Qué tiempo hace en Wáshington? _____

5. ¿Qué tiempo hace en Portland? _____

6. ¿Qué tiempo hace en Miami? _____

EXERCISE F   **Hacemos esto.**   Tell what the following people do using an idiomatic expression with *hacer*.

1. Mis abuelos deben estar en el aeropuerto antes de las cinco de la tarde. Ellos _____

_____ .

2. Antes de vestirse cada día mi hermana quiere _____

_____ .

3. Cuando los niños no saben algo, ellos _____

_____ .

4. Nosotros queremos ver a nuestros primos. Nosotros _____

_____ .

5. A mi hermano no le gusta cuando un bebé llora. Siempre le dice al bebé: _____

_____ .

b. Expressions with *DAR*

dar la hora	*to strike the hour*
El reloj *da las ocho.*	*The clock strikes eight.*
dar las gracias	*to thank*
Dan las gracias **al dependiente.**	*They thank the store clerk.*
dar un paseo	*to take a walk*
Tú *das un paseo* **cada mañana.**	*You take a walk each morning.*
darse la mano	*to shake hands*
Nosotros *nos damos la mano.*	*We shake hands.*

c. Other Idiomatic Verbal Expressions

acabar de + infinitive	*to have just*
Ella *acaba de salir.*	*She has just left.*
dejar caer	*to drop*
La señora *dejó caer* **dos monedas.**	*The woman dropped two coins.*
dejar de + infinitive	*to fail to; to stop; to neglect to*
Ellos *dejan de trabajar.*	*They stop working.*
echar al correo	*to mail*
Echo la tarjeta **al correo.**	*I mail the card.*
echar de menos	*to miss (a person or thing)*
Echo de menos **a mis amigos.**	*I miss my friends.*
estar de acuerdo	*to agree*
Ellos *están de acuerdo.*	*They agree.*
guardar cama	*to stay in bed*
Ella *guarda cama* **por un día.**	*She stays in bed for one day.*
llegar a ser	*to become; to get to be*
Él quiere *llegar a ser* **astronauta.**	*He wants to be an astronaut.*
pensar + infinitive	*to intend to*
Ella *piensa trabajar* **en un banco.**	*She intends to work in a bank.*
querer decir	*to mean*
¿Qué *quiere decir* «**ausente**»?	*What does "ausente" mean?*
sacar una fotografía	*to take a picture*
Yo *saco* **muchas** *fotografías.*	*I take many pictures.*

EXERCISE G   **Noticias familares** (Family news)   At a family reunion, everyone is anxious to catch up on the family news. Complete each statement with an expression from those listed below and write its appropriate form in the space provided.

acabar de	dejar caer	guardar cama
dar	dejar de	llegar a ser
dar la mano	echar de menos	pensar
dar las gracias	echarlas al correo	querer decir
dar un paseo	estar de acuerdo	sacar fotografías

1. Sarita busca otro novio porque ella _____ pelear con Felipe.

2. Tía Laura está enferma y debe _____ por varios días.

3. Norma está muy contenta porque trabaja en una tienda de ropa y ella quiere _____ diseñadora de ropa.

4. Mi abuela quiere bajar de peso. Ella va a _____ comer chocolates.

5. Enrique no está presente y todos lo _____ .

6. Janet escribió las invitaciones a su boda. Ahora ella tiene que _____ .

7. La novia de Jaime es muy torpe. Siempre ella _____ algo.

8. Mi padre y su hermano siempre pelean. Ellos nunca _____ .

9. Mi mamá siempre lleva su cámara y _____ de la familia.

10. Mi familia es muy puntual. Todos llegan cuando el reloj _____ las dos.

11. Emily y Alan reciben muchos regalos por su compromiso. Ahora ellos tienen que

   _____ .

12. Mi primo Eddy es muy formal porque siempre _____ al saludar a una persona.

13. A mis tíos les fascina _____ por el parque después de comer.

14. Héctor tiene el catálogo de una universidad en Salamanca porque él _____ estudiar allí durante el verano.

15. El hijo de Silvia aprende a hablar y siempre pregunta «¿ _____ ?» cuando no comprende algo.

EXERCISE H   **Preguntas**   Answer these questions a friend asks you.

1. ¿Haces muchas preguntas en todas tus clases?

   _____

2. ¿A quién echas de menos durante las vacaciones de verano?

   _____

3. ¿Piensas tomar otro curso durante el verano?

_____

4. ¿Das las gracias a las personas que te ayudan?

_____

5. ¿A qué hora dejas de ver la televisión cada noche?

_____

6. ¿Sacas fotografías de tus compañeros de clase?

_____

7. ¿Das un paseo todos los días?

_____

8. ¿Acabas de alquilar una película buena?

_____

9. ¿Siempre estás de acuerdo con tus padres?

_____

10. ¿Quieres llegar a ser arquitecto?

_____

 **EXERCISE I**   **Mi círculo de amigos** (My circle of friends)   Write ten sentences in which you tell something about each of the friends in your group. Use as many idiomatic verbal expressions as possible.

_____

_____

_____

_____

_____

_____

_____

_____

Appendix

1. Regular Verbs

INFINITIVE	cant**ar**	beb**er**	abr**ir**
PRESENT	cant**o**	beb**o**	abr**o**
	cant**as**	beb**es**	abr**es**
	cant**a**	beb**e**	abr**e**
	cant**amos**	beb**emos**	abr**imos**
	cant**áis**	beb**éis**	abr**ís**
	cant**an**	beb**en**	abr**en**
PRETERIT	cant**é**	beb**í**	abr**í**
	cant**aste**	beb**iste**	abr**iste**
	cant**ó**	beb**ió**	abr**ió**
	cant**amos**	beb**imos**	abr**imos**
	cant**asteis**	beb**isteis**	abr**isteis**
	cant**aron**	beb**ieron**	abr**ieron**
COMMANDS	cant**a** no cant**es** } (tú)	beb**e** no beb**as** } (tú)	abr**e** no abr**as** } (tú)
	cant**e** (Ud.)	beb**a** (Ud.)	abr**a** (Ud.)
	cant**emos** (nosotros)	beb**amos** (nosotros)	abr**amos** (nosotros)
	cant**ad** no cant**éis** } (vosotros)	beb**ed** no beb**áis** } (vosotros)	abr**id** no abr**áis** } (vosotros)
	cant**en** (Uds.)	beb**an** (Uds.)	abr**an** (Uds.)

2. Stem-Changing Verbs

a. Stem-Change *O* to *UE*

INFINITIVE	mostrar (**o** to **ue**)	volv**er** (**o** to **ue**)	jug**ar** (**u** to **ue**)
PRESENT	m**ue**stro	v**ue**lvo	j**ue**go
	m**ue**stras	v**ue**lves	j**ue**gas
	m**ue**stra	v**ue**lve	j**ue**ga
	mostramos	volvemos	jugamos
	mostráis	volvéis	jugáis
	m**ue**stran	v**ue**lven	j**ue**gan

COMMANDS	muestra no muestres } (tú)	vuelve no vuelvas } (tú)	juega no juegues } (tú)
	muestre (Ud.)	vuelva (Ud.)	juegue (Ud.)
	mostremos (nosotros)	volvamos (nosotros)	juguemos (nosotros)
	mostrad no mostréis } (vosotros)	volved no volváis } (vosotros)	jugad no juguéis } (vosotros)
	muestren (Uds.)	vuelvan (Uds.)	jueguen (Uds.)

b. Stem-Change E to IE

INFINITIVE	pensar (e to ie)	perder (e to ie)	sentir (e to ie)
PRESENT	pienso piensas piensa pensamos pensáis piensan	pierdo pierdes pierde perdemos perdéis pierden	siento sientes siente sentimos sentís sienten
COMMANDS	piensa no pienses } (tú)	pierde no pierdas } (tú)	siente no sientas } (tú)
	piense (Ud.)	pierda (Ud.)	sienta (Ud.)
	pensemos (nosotros)	perdamos (nosotros)	sintamos (nosotros)
	pensad no penséis } (vosotros)	perded no perdáis } (vosotros)	sentid no sintáis } (vosotros)
	piensen (Uds.)	pierdan (Uds.)	sientan (Uds.)

c. Stem-Change E to I

INFINITIVE	PRESENT	COMMANDS
pedir (e to i)	pido pides	pide no pidas } (tú)
	pide	pida (Ud.)
	pedimos	pidamos (nosotros)
	pedís	pedid no pidáis } (tú)
	pidan	pidan (Uds.)

3. Spelling-Changing Verbs

a. Infinitives in *-cer* or *-cir*

INFINITIVE	PRESENT	COMMANDS
ofrec**er** (**c** to **zc**)	ofre**zc**o ofreces	ofrece no ofre**zc**as } (tú)
	ofrece	ofre**zc**a (Ud.)
	ofrecemos	ofre**zc**amos (nosotros)
	ofrecéis	ofreced no ofre**zc**áis } (vosotros)
	ofrecen	ofre**zc**an (Uds.)
conduc**ir** (**c** to **zc**)	condu**zc**o conduces	conduce no condu**zc**as } (tú)
	conduce	condu**zc**a (Ud.)
	conducimos	condu**zc**amos (nosotros)
	conducís	conducid no condu**zc**áis } (vosotros)
	conducen	condu**zc**an (Uds.)

4. Irregular Verbs

NOTE: Only the tenses containing irregular forms are given.

INFINITIVE	PRESENT	COMMANDS
ha**c**er	ha**g**o haces	ha**z** no ha**g**as } (tú)
	hace	ha**g**a (Ud.)
	hacemos	ha**g**amos (nosotros)
	hacéis	haced no ha**g**áis } (vosotros)
	hacen	ha**g**an (Uds.)

INFINITIVE	PRESENT	COMMANDS
ir	**voy** **vas**	**ve** no **vayas** } (tú)
	va	**vaya** (Ud.)
	vamos	**vay**amos (nosotros)
	vais	id no vayáis } (vosotros)
	van	**vay**an (Uds.)
oír	oigo oyes	oye no oigas } (tú)
	oye	oiga Ud.
	oímos	oigamos (nosotros)
	oís	oíd no oigáis } (vosotros)
	oyen	oigan (Uds.)
poner	pongo pones	pon no pongas } (tú)
	pone	ponga (Ud.)
	ponemos	pongamos (nosotros)
	ponéis	poned no pongáis } (vosotros)
	ponen	pongan (Uds.)
saber	sé sabes	sabe no sepas } (tú)
	sabe	sepa (Ud.)
	sabemos	sepamos (nosotros)
	sabéis	sabed no sepáis } (vosotros)
	saben	sepan (Uds.)

INFINITIVE	PRESENT	COMMANDS
sal**ir**	sal**go** sales	sal no sal**gas** } (tú)
	sale	sal**ga** (Ud.)
	salimos	sal**gamos** (nosotros)
	salís	salid no sal**gáis** } (vosotros)
	salen	sal**gan** (Uds.)
s**er**	s**oy** **er**es	s**é** no seas } (tú)
	es	sea (Ud.)
	s**o**mos	seamos (nosotros)
	s**o**is	sed no seáis } (vosotros)
	s**on**	sean (Uds.)
ten**er**	ten**go** t**ie**nes	ten no ten**gas** } (tú)
	t**ie**ne	ten**ga** (Ud.)
	tenemos	ten**gamos** (nosotros)
	tenéis	tened no ten**gáis** } (vosotros)
	t**ie**nen	ten**gan** (Uds.)
tra**er**	tra**igo** traes	trae no tra**igas** } (tú)
	trae	tra**iga** (Ud.)
	traemos	tra**igamos** (nosotros)
	traéis	traed no tra**igáis** } (vosotros)
	traen	tra**igan** (Uds.)

INFINITIVE	PRESENT	COMMANDS
venir	vengo vienes	ven no vengas } (tú)
	viene	venga (Ud.)
	venimos	vengamos
	venís	venid no vengáis } (vosotros)
	vienen	vengan (Uds.)
ver	veo ves	ve no veas } (tú)
	ve	vea (Ud.)
	vemos	veamos (nosotros)
	veis	ved no veáis } (vosotros)
	ven	vean (Uds.)

5.   Punctuation

Although Spanish punctuation is similar to English, it has the following major differences:

a. In Spanish, questions have an inverted question mark (¿) at the beginning and a normal one at the end.

¿Quién es?   *Who is it?*

b. In Spanish, exclamatory sentences have an inverted exclamation point (¡) at the beginning and a normal one at the end.

¡Qué día!   *What a day!*

c. Commas are used to separate a nonrestrictive relative clause.

La blusa, que costó muchísimo,   *The blouse, which cost*
es muy bonita.   *a lot, is very pretty.*

d. The comma is not used before *y, e, o, u,* and *ni* in a series.

El lunes, el martes y el miércoles   *There are classes on Monday,*
hay clases.   *Tuesday, and Wednesday.*

e. With decimals, Spanish uses a comma where English uses a period.

3,5 (tres coma cinco)   *3.5 (three point five)*

f. Spanish final quotation marks precede the comma or period.

Cervantes escribió «El Quijote».   *Cervantes wrote "The Quijote."*

6. Syllabication

Spanish words are generally divided at the end of a line according to units of sound.

a. A syllable normally begins with a consonant. The division is made before the consonant.

te / **n**er   di / **n**e / ro   a / **m**e / **r**i / ca / no   re / **f**e / **r**ir

b. **Ch, ll,** and **rr** are never divided.

pe / **rr**o   ha / **ll**a / do   di / **ch**o

c. If two or more consonants are combined, the division is made before the last consonant, except in the combinations **bl, br, cl, cr, pl, pr,** and **tr.**

trans / **p**or / te   des / cu / **b**ier / to   con / **t**i / nuar   al / **b**er / ca

BUT:

ha/**bl**ar   a/**br**ir   des/**cr**i/bir   a/**pr**en/der   dis/**tr**i/buir

d. Compound words, including words with prefixes and suffixes, may be divided by components or by syllables.

sur / a / me / ri / ca / no   OR   **su** / **ra** / me / ri / ca / no

mal / estar   OR   **ma** / **les** / tar

7. Pronunciation

Stress in a word follows three general rules:

a. If the word ends in a vowel, *n,* or *s,* the next-to-last syllable is stressed.

es / **cue** / la   de/**sas**/tre   **jo**/ven   se/**ño**/res

b. If the word ends in a consonant, except *n or* s, the final syllable is stressed.

com/pren/**der**   a/la/**bar**   re/ci/**bir**   se/**ñor**

c. All exceptions to the above have a written accent mark.

sá/ba/do   **jó**/ve/nes   A/**dán**   **Cé**/sar   fran/**cés**

Spanish-English Vocabulary

The Spanish-English Vocabulary is intended to be complete for the context of this book.

Nouns are listed in the singular. Regular feminine forms of nouns are indicated by **(-a)** or the ending that replaces the masculine ending: **amigo(-a)** or **consejero(-era)**. Irregular feminine forms of nouns are given in full: **héroe** *m.* hero (*f.* **heroína** heroine). Regular feminine forms of adjectives are indicated by **-a**.

ABBREVIATIONS

adj.	adjective	*irr.*	irregular
aux.	auxiliary verb	*m.*	masculine
f.	feminine	*pl.*	plural
inf.	infinitive	*sing.*	singular

abogado(-a) lawyer
abrigo *m.* overcoat
abuela *f.* grandmother
abuelo *m.* grandfather
aburrido, -a boring
acabar to end;
  acabar de to have just
aceite *m.* oil
acero *m.* steel
acompañar to accompany
acostado, -a lying down
acróbata *m. & f.* acrobat
actividad *f.* activity
acuario *m.* aquarium
acuerdo *m.* agreement;
  estar de acuerdo to agree
adivinanza *f.* riddle
adorno *m.* decoration
aeropuerto *m.* airport
aficionado(-a) fan
ahí there
ahora now; **ahora mismo**
  right now
ahorrar to save
aire *m.* air
ajedrez *m.* chess
alegre *m. & f. adj.* happy

alemán *m.* German
  (language); *also adj.*
  alemán, -ana German
alfabeto *m.* alphabet
alfombra *f.* rug, carpet
algo something
algodón *m.* cotton
alguien someone
alguno, -a some, any
allí there
almacén *m.* department store
almorzar (ue) to eat lunch
almuerzo *m.* lunch
alquilar to rent
alto, -a tall
alumno(-a) student
amable *m. & f. adj.* nice
amar to love
amarillo, -a yellow
ambiente *m.* atmosphere;
medio ambiente environment
amigo(-a) friend
amplio, -a large, ample
anaranjado, -a orange
andar to walk
anillo *m.* ring
animado, -a animated, lively

año *m.* year
anoche last night
ansioso, -a anxious
anteayer the day before
  yesterday
anteojos *m. pl.* eyeglasses
antes de before
antiguo, -a old
anuncio *m.* announcement, ad
apagado, -a shut off
apagar to put out, extinguish
apoyar to support
aprender to learn
aquel that (*f.* **aquella**);
  aquellos, aquellas those)
aquí here
árbol *m.* tree
arena *f.* sand
arete *m.* earring
armario *m.* closet
arquitecto(-a) architect
arreglar to arrange, fix;
  to straighten up
arroz *m.* rice
asado *m.* roast; *also adj.*
  asado, -a roasted
asamblea *f.* assembly

ascensor *m.* elevator
asiento *m.* seat
asistir (a) to attend
aspiradora *f.* vacuum cleaner
aspirina *f.* aspirin
aula *f.* **(el aula)** classroom
autobús *m.* bus
autor(-ora) author
avión *m.* airplane
ayer yesterday
ayudar to help
azul *m. & f. adj.* blue

bailar to dance
baile *m.* dance
bajar to go down, descend;
   to lower
baloncesto *m.* basketball
banco *m.* bank
barato, -a cheap, inexpensive
barbacoa *f.* barbecue
barco *m.* boat
barrer to sweep
basura *f.* garbage, trash
batido *m.* shake; *also adj.*
   batido, -a shaken, whipped
beca *f.* scholarship
béisbol *m.* baseball
biblioteca *f.* library
bicicleta *f.* bicycle
billar *m.* billiards
blanco, -a white
boca *f.* mouth
boda *f.* wedding
boleto *m.* ticket
boliche *m.* bowling
bolígrafo *m.* ballpoint pen
bolsa *f.* handbag, purse
bombero(-era) firefighter
bondadoso, -a kind
bonito, -a pretty
bosque *m.* forest
bota *f.* boot
botánico, -a botanical
botella *f.* bottle
brazo *m.* arm

broma *f.* joke; prank
broncear to tan
bufanda *f.* scarf
buscar to look for

cabeza *f.* head
cada each, every
cadena *f.* chain
caer to fall
cafetería *f.* cafeteria
caja *f.* box; cashier
calendario *m.* calendar
caliente *m. & f. adj.* warm, hot
calle *f.* street
cama *f.* bed
cámara *f.* camera
cambiar to change, exchange
cambio *m.* change
caminar to walk
camión *m.* truck
camiseta *f.* T-shirt
campamento *m.* camp
campo *m.* country
cancha *f.* court; **cancha**
   de tenis tennis court
canción *f.* song
candidato(-a) candidate
cantar to sing
capítulo *m.* chapter
cara *f.* face
caricatura *f.* cartoon
carne *f.* meat
caro, -a expensive
carrera *f.* race
carro *m.* car
carrusel *m.* carousel
carta *f.* letter
cartel *m.* poster
cartera *f.* billfold
casarse to get married
cebra *f.* zebra
celebrar to celebrate
cenar to have supper
centro *m.* center; downtown;
   centro comercial *m.* mall,
   shopping center

cepillo *m.* brush; **cepillo**
   de dientes toothbrush
cerca (de) near
cerdo *m.* pig, pork
cerrar (ie) to close
césped *m.* lawn; grass
chaleco *m.* vest
charla *f.* chat
charlar to chat
chico(-a) boy; girl; *also adj.* small
chimenea *f.* fireplace
chiste *m.* joke
chuleta *f.* chop
cielo *m.* sky
ciencia *f.* science
científico(-a) scientist
cine *m.* movie theater, movies
cinturón *m.* belt
circo *m.* circus
círculo *m.* circle
cita *f.* appointment
ciudad *f.* city
clase *f.* class; kind
clásico, -a classical
clima *m.* climate
cocina *f.* kitchen
cocinar to cook
codo *m.* elbow
colchón *m.* mattress
coleccionar to collect
colgar (ue) to hang
comandante *m. & f.*
   commander, chief
comedor *m.* dining room
comenzar (ie) to begin, start
cómico, -a funny
comida *f.* food; meal
comienzo *m.* beginning
como as, like;
   ¿cómo? how?, what?
cómodo, -a comfortable
compacto, -a compact;
   disco compacto *m.* compact
   disk (CD)
compañero(-era) companion,
   classmate

compartir to share

complejo, -a complex

comprar to buy

compromiso *m.* engagement

concierto *m.* concert

concurso *m.* contest, game show

confundido, -a confused

congelado, -a frozen

congelador *m.* freezer

congreso *m.* convention

conocer (zc) to know (a person); to be acquainted (with)

consejero(-era) counselor

construcción *f.* construction

construir to construct, build

contado *m.* cash; **pagar al contado** to pay cash

contaminar to contaminate

contar (ue) to count; to relate, tell

contento, -a happy

contestar to answer

contrato *m.* contract

copa *f.* wine glass

copiar to copy

corbata *f.* tie

coro *m.* chorus

correo *m.* mail; post office; **correo electrónico** electronic mail

correr to run

cortar to cut

corte *f.* court

cortesía *f.* courtesy

corto, -a short

cosa *f.* thing

costar (ue) to cost

costumbre *f.* custom

creer to believe

cuaderno *m.* notebook

cuadra *f.* block

cuadro *m.* painting, picture; square; **a cuadros** plaid

cualquier any

cuando when; **¿cuándo?** when?

cuánto, -a how much; **¿cuántos, -as?** how many

cuarto *m.* room; quarter, fourth

cubrir to cover

cucharita *f.* teaspoon

cuchillo *m.* knife

cuenta *f.* bill, check

cuento *m.* story

cuero *m.* leather

cuidadosamente carefully

cuidado *m.* care; **tener cuidado** to be careful

cuidar to take care of

cumpleaños *m. sing. & pl.* birthday

curso *m.* course

dálmata *m. & f. adj.* Dalmatian

dama *f.* lady; **jugar a las damas** to play checkers

debajo de under, beneath

deber to be supposed to

decidir to decide

decir to say, tell

decorar to decorate

dedo *m.* finger

defender (ie) defend

dejar to leave; to allow; **dejar de** to fail to; to stop; to neglect to; **dejar caer** to drop

delante de in front of

delgado, -a thin

delicioso, -a delicious

demasiado, -a too much

dentista *m. & f.* dentist

dentro de within

deporte *m.* sport

deportista *m. & f.* athlete

deportivo, -a sport (*adj.*)

desayuno *m.* breakfast

descansar to rest

descortés *m. & f. adj.* impolite

describir to describe

descubrir to discover

desear to wish, want

desechable disposable

desfile *m.* parade

desilusionado, -a disillusioned

deslizador *m.* scooter

despacio slow

después de after

detrás de behind

devolver (ue) to return, give back

día *m.* day; **día de fiesta** *m.* holiday; **todos los días** everyday

diálogo *m.* dialog

diario daily

dibujar to draw

dibujo *m.* drawing, sketch; **dibujos animados** cartoons

diccionario *m.* dictionary

difícil *m. & f. adj.* difficult

diligente *m. & f. adj.* diligent

dinero *m.* money

dirección *f.* address

director(-ora) director; principal

disco *m.* record, disk

disculpa *f.* excuse, apology; **pedir disculpas** to ask for forgiveness, apologize

diseñador(-ora) designer

diseñar to design

disfrutar to enjoy

divertido, -a amusing, fun

dividir to divide

docena *f.* dozen

documental *m.* documentary

doler (ue) to be painful, to cause sorrow

dolor *m.* pain; **tener dolor de...** to have a(n) __ ache

dominar to dominate

domingo *m.* Sunday

donde where; **¿dónde?** where?

dormir (ue) to sleep

dueño(-a) owner

dulce sweet; **dulces** *m. pl.* candies, sweets

durante during

durar to last
duro, -a hard

echar to throw; **echar al correo** to mail
ecuatoriano, -a Ecuadorian
edificio *m.* building
ejemplo *m.* example; **por ejemplo** for example
ejercicio *m.* exercise
elecciones *f. pl.* election
empezar (ie) to begin, start
empleado(-ada) employee
encantar to delight, to like a lot
encendido, -a lighted
encima de on, on top of
encontrar (ue) to find
encuesta *f.* survey
enfermo, -a sick, ill
ensalada *f.* salad
ensayo *m.* rehearsal
enseñar to teach
entender (ie) to understand
entrada *f.* entrance; admission
entrar (en) to enter (into)
entre between
entregar to deliver, submit
entrenador(-ora) trainer
entretener to entertain
envuelto, -a wrapped
equipo *m.* team
equitación *f.* (horseback) riding
escalera *f.* staircase
escolar school (*adj.*);
   autobús escolar school bus
escribir to write
escritorio *m.* desk
escuchar to listen (to)
escuela *f.* school
ese, -a that (*pl.* **esos, -as** those)
eso that; **por eso** that's why
español *m.* Spanish (language); *also adj.*
   español, -a Spanish
esperar to wait; to hope
esquiador(-ora) skier

esquiar to ski
estadio *m.* stadium
estante *m.* shelf
estatua *f.* statue
este, -a this; (*pl.* **estos, -as** these)
estilo *m.* style
estómago *m.* stomach
estrecho, -a narrow
estrella *f.* star
estreno *m.* opening
estricto, -a strict
estudiante *m. & f.* student
estudiantil *m. & f. adj.* student;
   consejo estudiantil student council
estudiar to study
excursión *f.* excursion, trip
explicar to explain
extranjero, -a foreign
extraño, -a strange

fácil *m. & f. adj.* easy
falda *f.* skirt
faltar to be lacking, to need
familia *f.* family
famoso, -a famous
fantasía *f.* fantasy
fascinar to delight, to like a lot
favor *m.* favor; **por favor** please
felicidades *f. pl.* congratulations
feliz happy
feo, -a ugly
fiesta *f.* party
fin *m.* end; **por fin** at last, finally
firmar to sign
físico, -a physical
flauta *f.* flute
flor *f.* flower
florería *f.* flower shop
formulario *m.* form
fotografía *f.* photograph
francés *m.* French (language); *also adj.* **francés, francesa** French

frase *f.* sentence
frecuencia *f.* frequency
frente a facing
fresa *f.* strawberry
frijol *m.* bean
frío, -a cold
fruta *f.* fruit
fuego *m.* fire
fuerte *m. & f. adj.* strong
función *f.* performance, show
funcionar to function; perform
fútbol *m.* soccer; **fútbol americano** *m.* football

galleta *f.* cracker;
   galletita *f.* cookie
ganar to earn; to win
garganta *f.* throat
gastar to spend
gato(-a) cat
gemelo(-a) twin
gimnasio *m.* gym
globo *m.* balloon
gobierno *m.* government
goma *f.* eraser
gorra *f.* cap
grabadora *f.* recorder
gracias *f. pl.* thank you;
   dar las gracias to thank
graduarse to graduate
grande *m. & f. adj.* large, big
gris *m. & f. adj.* gray
gritar to shout
grito *m.* shout
grueso, -a thick
guante *m.* glove
guardar to keep; **guardar cama** to stay in bed
guía *m. & f.* guide; guidebook (*f. noun only*)
guitarra *f.* guitar
gustar to like

hábilmente skillfully
hablar to speak
hacer to make, do

hacha *f.* **(el hacha)** ax
hambre *f.* **(el hambre)** hunger;
  tener hambre to be hungry
hasta until
hay there is, there are; **no hay**
  más remedio it can't be
  helped
helado *m.* ice cream; *also adj.*
  helado, -a iced
hermana *f.* sister
hermano *m.* brother;
  hermanos brothers; siblings
héroe *m.* hero (*f.* **heroína**
  heroine)
hielo *m.* ice
hija *f.* daughter
hijo *m.* son; **hijos** sons; children
hoja *f.* leaf
hombre *m.* man
horno *m.* oven; **horno de**
  microondas microwave oven
hoy today
huarache *m.* sandal
hueso *m.* bone

idioma *m.* language
iglesia *f.* church
incendio *m.* fire
independiente *m. & f. adj.*
  independent
informática *f.* computer science
ingeniero(-era) engineer
inglés *m.* English (language);
  also adj. **inglés, -esa** English
insistir (en) to insist on
inteligente *m. & f. adj.*
  intelligent
invitar to invite
ir to go; **ir de compras** to go
  shopping
italiano *m.* Italian (language);
  also adj. **italiano, -a** Italian
izquierdo, -a left

jabón *m.* soap
jamás never, not ever

japonés *m.* Japanese; *also adj.*
  japonés, japonesa Japanese
jardín *m.* garden
jirafa *f.* giraffe
joven *m. & f.* young person;
  also m. & f. adj. young
juego *m.* game
jueves *m.* Thursday
jugo *m.* juice
juguete *m.* toy
junto, -a together

lado *m.* side; **al lado de** next to
lago *m.* lake
lamentar to regret
lámpara *f.* lamp
lana *f.* wool
lápiz *m.* pencil
largo, -a long
lavadora *f.* washing machine
lavaplatos *m. sing.* dishwasher
lavar to wash
lección *f.* lesson
leche *f.* milk
lechero(-era) milk delivery
  person
lechuga *f.* lettuce
leer to read
legumbre *f.* vegetable
lejos far; **lejos de** far from
lentes *m. pl.* eye glasses
león *m.* lion (*f.* **leona** lioness)
licuadora *f.* blender
limonada *f.* lemonade
limpiar to clean
limpio, -a clean
lino *m.* linen
líquido *m.* liquid
listo, -a ready; **estar listo, -a**
  to be ready; **ser listo, -a** to be
  clever, smart
llamada *f.* call
llamar to call; **llamarse: me**
  llamo... my name is . . .
llanto *m.* cry
llave *f.* key

llegar to arrive
llevar to carry; to take; to wear
llover (ue) to rain
locutor(-ora) announcer
lucha *f.* fight; **lucha libre** *f.*
  wrestling
lugar *m.* place; **tener lugar**
  to take place
lunes *m.* Monday
luz *f.* light

madre *f.* mother
maestro(-a) teacher
mago(-a) magician
maleta *f.* suitcase
mañana *f.* morning; **esta**
  mañana this morning;
  also adv. tomorrow; **pasado**
  mañana the day after
  tomorrow
mandar to send
mano *f.* hand
mantel *m.* tablecloth
mantequilla *f.* butter
manzana *f.* apple
maquillaje *m.* makeup
máquina *f.* machine
mar *m.* sea
maratón *m.* marathon
marcador *m.* marker
marcar to dial
martes *m.* Tuesday
más more; **no puedo más**
  I can't take any more.
máscara *f.* mask
mayor greater, older
mecánico(-a) mechanic
mediano, -a medium
medianoche *f.* midnight
medicina *f.* medicine
médico(-a) doctor
medio, -a half
mediodía *m.* noon, midday
medir (i) to measure
mejor better
menor lesser, younger

menos less; **echar de menos** to miss; **por lo menos** at least

mensaje *m.* message

mentira *f.* lie

mercancía *f.* merchandise

mermelada *f.* marmalade, jam

mesa *f.* table

mesera *f.* waitress

mesero *m.* waiter

meter to put

metro *m.* subway

mexicano, -a Mexican

miedo *m.* fear; **tener miedo de** to be afraid of

mientras while

miércoles *m.* Wednesday

milla *f.* mile

mirar to look (at)

mismo, -a same

mochila *f.* knapsack

mojado, -a wet

molino *m.* mill; **molino de pimienta** peppermill

moneda *f.* coin

monopatín *m.* skateboard

montaña *f.* mountain

montar to ride (a bicycle, horse)

monumento *m.* monument

morado, -a purple

morir (ue) to die

mostrar (ue) to show

mueble *m.* furniture

muela *f.* molar (tooth)

mujer *f.* woman

muñeca *f.* doll

museo *m.* museum

música *f.* music

nacer (zc) to be born

nacionalidad *f.* nationality

nada nothing; **de nada** you're welcome

nadar to swim

nadie no one

naranja *f.* orange

natación *f.* swimming

necesitar to need

negro, -a black

nervioso, -a nervous

nevar (ie) to snow

nieta *f.* granddaughter

nieto *m.* grandson

niñez *f.* childhood

ninguno, -a no, none, (not) any

niña *f.* girl

niño *m.* boy

noche *f.* night; **de la noche** P.M.; **esta noche** tonight; **anoche** last night

nombre *m.* name

noticia *f. news item*; **noticias** news

noticiero *m.* news broadcast

novia *f.* girlfriend

novio *m.* boyfriend

nube *f.* cloud

nublado, -a cloudy

nuevo, -a new

número *m.* number; shoe size

nunca never

obedecer (zc) to obey

obra *f.* work

ocupado, -a busy

oficio *m.* job, trade, position

oír to hear; to listen

ojo *m.* eye

ola *f.* wave

olvidar to forget

organizado, -a organized

orgulloso, -a proud

oro *m.* gold

oscuro, -a dark

oso *m.* bear

paciencia *f.* patience

padre *m.* father; **padres** fathers; parents

pagar to pay (for)

país *m.* country

paisaje *m.* landscape

pájaro *m.* bird

palabra *f.* word

palacio *m.* palace

pálido, -a pale

palomitas (de maíz) *f.* popcorn

pan *m.* bread

pantalones *m. pl.* pants, trousers

pañuelo *m.* handkerchief

papa *f.* potato; **papas fritas** french fries

papel *m.* paper

pardo, -a brown

parecer to seem

pared *f.* wall

parque *m.* park; **parque de bomberos** fire house

párrafo *m.* paragraph

parte *f.* part, section

partido *m.* game

partir to leave

pasado,-a past; **pasado mañana** the day after tomorrow

pasaporte *m.* passport

pasar to pass; to spend (time)

pasatiempo *m.* hobby, pastime

paseo *m.* walk

patín *m.* skate

patinaje *m.* skating

patinar to skate

pavo *m.* turkey

payaso(-a) clown

pedir (i) to ask for, request; to order (food)

pelear to fight

película *f.* film

peligro *m.* danger

pelo *m.* hair

pelota *f.* ball

peluche *m.* stuffed animal (*toy*)

pensar (ie) to think

peor worse

pequeño, -a small

perder (ie) to lose; to waste; to miss (bus, train)

periódico *m.* newspaper

permiso *m.* permission

permitir to permit, allow

perro *m.* dog

pescado *m.* fish

pie *m.* foot

piel *f.* leather

pierna *f.* leg

piloto *m. & f.* pilot

piña *f.* pineapple

pintar to paint

pintor(-ora) *m.* painter

pintura *f.* painting

pisapapeles *m. sing. & pl.* paper weight

piscina *f.* pool

piso *m.* floor

pizarra *f.* chalkboard

plan *m.* plan

plancha *f.* iron

plata *f.* silver

plátano *m.* plantain

plato *m.* plate

playa *f.* beach

poco little; **poco a poco** little by little

poder (ue) to be able; can, may

poesía *f.* poetry

pastel *m.* cake

político(-a) politician

pollo *m.* chicken

poner to put, place

porque because; **¿por qué?** why?

portátil *m. & f.* portable

portugués *m.* Portuguese (language); *also adj.*
   portugués, -esa Portuguese

postre *m.* dessert

practicar to practice

precio *m.* price

preferir (ie) to prefer

pregunta *f.* question

preguntar to ask

premio *m.* prize

prenda *f.* article (of clothing)

preocupado, -a worried

preparar to prepare

presidente(-a) president

prestar to lend; **prestar atención** to pay attention

presumir to boast

primero, -a first

primo(-a) cousin

prisa *f.* hurry, haste; **tener prisa** to be in a hurry

profesor(-ora) teacher

programador(-ora) programmer

progreso *m.* progress

promesa *f.* promise

prometer to promise

pronóstico *m.* forecast

pronto soon

propina *f.* tip

proteger to protect

próximo, -a next

proyecto *m.* project

puente *m.* bridge

puesto, -a put, set

pulsera *f.* bracelet

puma *m.* cougar

punto *m.* point; **en punto** sharp (time)

que who, whom, which, that; **¿qué?** what?, which?; **¡qué ...!** what a... !, how ...!

querer (ie) to want; to wish; to love

querido, -a dear

quien who, whom; **¿quién?** who?, whom?; **¿de quién?** whose?

rápido, -a fast, quick

raqueta *f.* racket

rato *m.* while; (short) time; **pasar un buen rato** to have a good time

ratoncito *m.* mouse

raya *f.* stripe; **a rayas** striped

razón *f.* reason; **tener razón** to be right

real *m. & f. adj.* royal; real

recibir to receive

reciclar to recycle

recoger to pick up, gather

reconocer (zc) to recognize

recordar (ue) to remember

recreo *m.* recreation

recuerdo *m.* remembrance, souvenir; **tienda de recuerdos** gift shop

redondo, -a round

referir (ie) to tell; to narrate

refresco *m.* soft drink, soda

refrigerador *m.* refrigerator

regalar to give a gift

regalo *m.* gift, present

regla *f.* rule

regresar to return

reloj *m.* watch, clock

remar to row

reñir (i) to quarrel; to scold

renovar (ue) to renew

reparar to repair

repetir (i) to repeat

resolver (ue) to solve

respetar to respect

responsable *m. & f. adj.* responsible

respuesta *f.* answer

retrato *m.* portrait

revista *f.* magazine

rinoceronte *m.* rhinoceros

risa *f.* laugh

rojo, -a red

rompecabezas *m. sing. & pl.* puzzle

ropa *f.* clothing

rosado, -a pink

ruina *f.* ruin

sábado *m.* Saturday

sábana *f.* sheet

saber to know

sabor *m.* flavor

sacar to take out; to take (photo)

sacudir to dust

sal *f.* salt

sala *f.* living room

salero *m.* salt shaker

salir to go out, leave

salón *m.* room; **salón de belleza** *m.* beauty shop

salsa *f.* sauce

saludar to greet

salvavidas *m. sing. & pl.* life preserver

sandalia *f.* sandal

santo(-a) saint

secadora *f.* clothes drier

sección *f.* section

secretario(-aria) secretary

sed *f.* thirst; **tener sed** to be thirsty

seda *f.* silk

seguir (i) to follow; continue

seguro, -a sure, safe

semana *f.* week

semejanza *f.* similarity

senador(-ora) senator

sentir (ie) to regret, be sorry; to feel

separar to separate

serio, -a serious

serpiente *f.* snake

servilleta *f.* napkin

servir (i) to serve

siempre always

siesta *f.* nap

siglo *m.* century

siguiente following; **al día siguiente** on the following day

silbar to whistle

silla *f.* chair

sillón *m.* chair

simpático, -a nice

sin without

sitio *m.* place

solo, -a alone

sombrero *m.* hat

sonrisa *f.* smile

sopa *f.* soup

sopera *f.* soup bowl

sorpresa *f.* surprise

sótano *m.* basement

suave *m & f. adj.* soft

subir to go up, climb; to raise

sucio, -a dirty

suelo *m.* ground

sueño *m.* sleep, dream; **tener sueño** to be sleepy

sufrir to suffer

supuesto: por supuesto of course

su(b)scripción *f.* subscription

tacaño, -a stingy

talla *f.* size

también *also*

tampoco neither, not either; **ni yo tampoco** me neither

tanteo *m.* score

tanto so much, as much; **no es para tanto** it's not such a big deal

tarde *f.* afternoon; **esta tarde** this afternoon; **de la tarde** P.M.; *also adv.* late

tarea *f.* chore, task, assignment

tarjeta *f.* card; **tarjeta postal** post card; **tarjeta de crédito** credit card

teatro *m.* theater

teléfono *m.* telephone

telenovela *f.* soap opera

televisor *m.* television set

temprano early

tenedor *m.* fork

tener to have

tenis *m.* tennis; **tenis** *m. pl.* sneakers

tercero, -a third

terminar to finish, end

tesorero(-era) treasurer

tía *f.* aunt

tío *m.* uncle

tiempo *m.* weather; time; **a tiempo** on time

tienda *f.* store

tierra *f.* land, earth

tiza *f.* chalk

toalla *f.* towel

tocadiscos *m. sing. & pl.* record player

tocador *m.* player; **tocador de discos compactos** CD player

tocar to touch; to play (a musical instrument); **tocar (a uno)** to be one's turn

tomar to take; to drink

torpe *m. & f. adj.* clumsy

tostadora *f.* toaster

trabajar to work

traje *m.* suit; **traje de baño** bathing suit

transporte *m.* transportation

tren *m.* train

trofeo *m.* trophy

turno *m.* turn

ubicación *f.* location

usar to use; to wear

útil *m. & f. adj.* useful; **útiles** *m. pl. noun* school supplies

vaca *f.* cow

vacaciones *f. pl.* vacation

vacío, -a empty

varios, -as various, several

vaso *m.* glass

vecino(-a) *f.* neighbor

vela *f.* candle
vender to sell
venir to come
ventana *f.* window
ver to see; to watch
verano *m.* summer
verdad *f.* truth; **¿verdad?** right?
verde *m. & f. adj.* green
verdura *f.* green, vegetable
vestido *m.* dress
veterinario(-aria) veterinarian

vez *f.* time; **de vez en cuando** from time to time
viajar to travel
vida *f.* life
videojuego *m.* videogame
viejo, -a old
viernes *m.* Friday
visita *f.* visit
visitar to visit
vivir to live
vivo, -a alive; **ser vivo, -a** to

be quick, smart
volar (ue) to fly
voleibol *m.* volleyball
volver (ue) to return, come (go) back
votar to vote
voz *f.* voice
vuelo *m.* flight

zanahoria *f.* carrot
zapato *m.* shoe